The Woodruffs
of
Cloud County, Kansas

Fifty Years of One of the Founding Families

DAVID HAYES

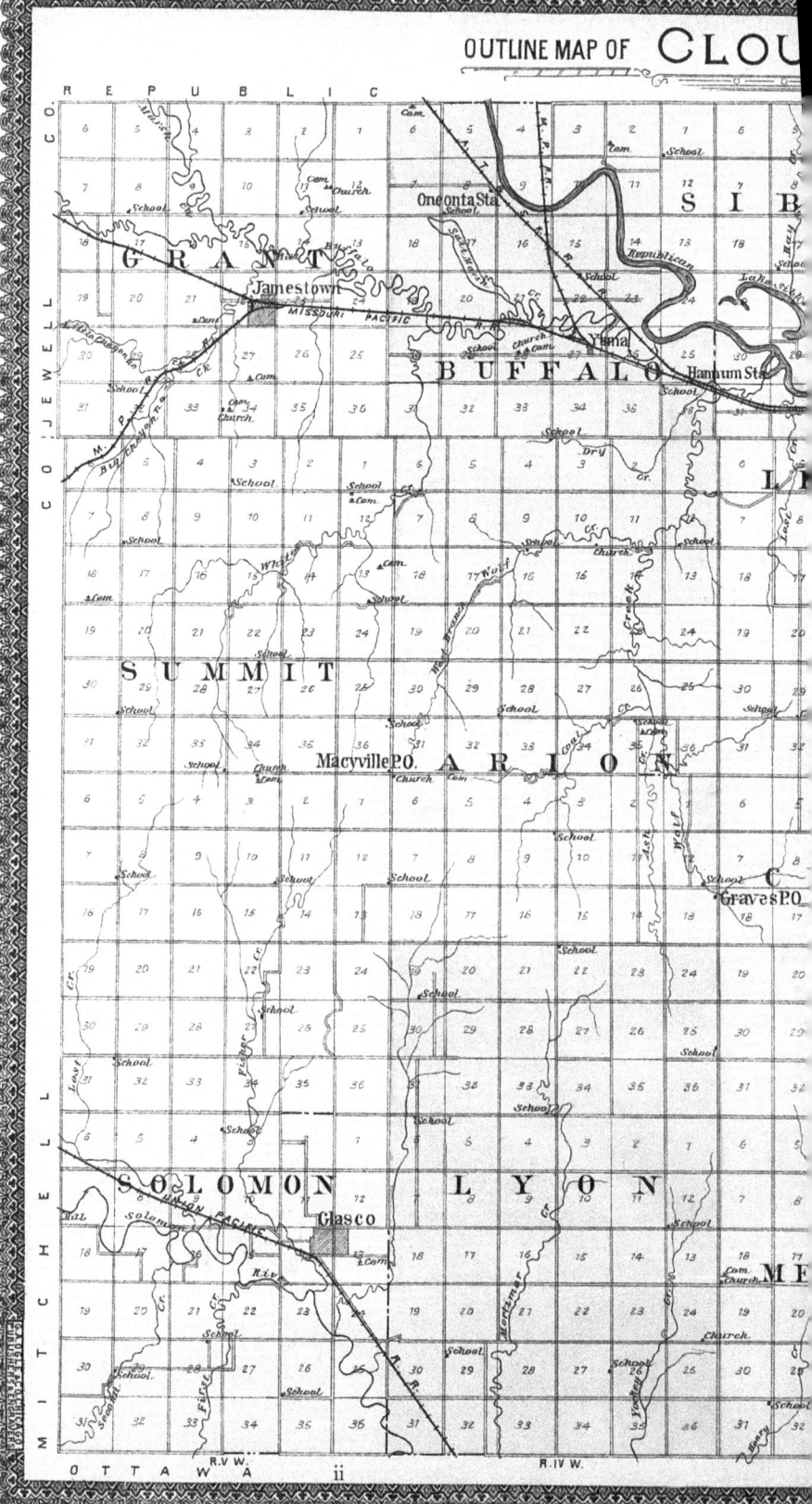

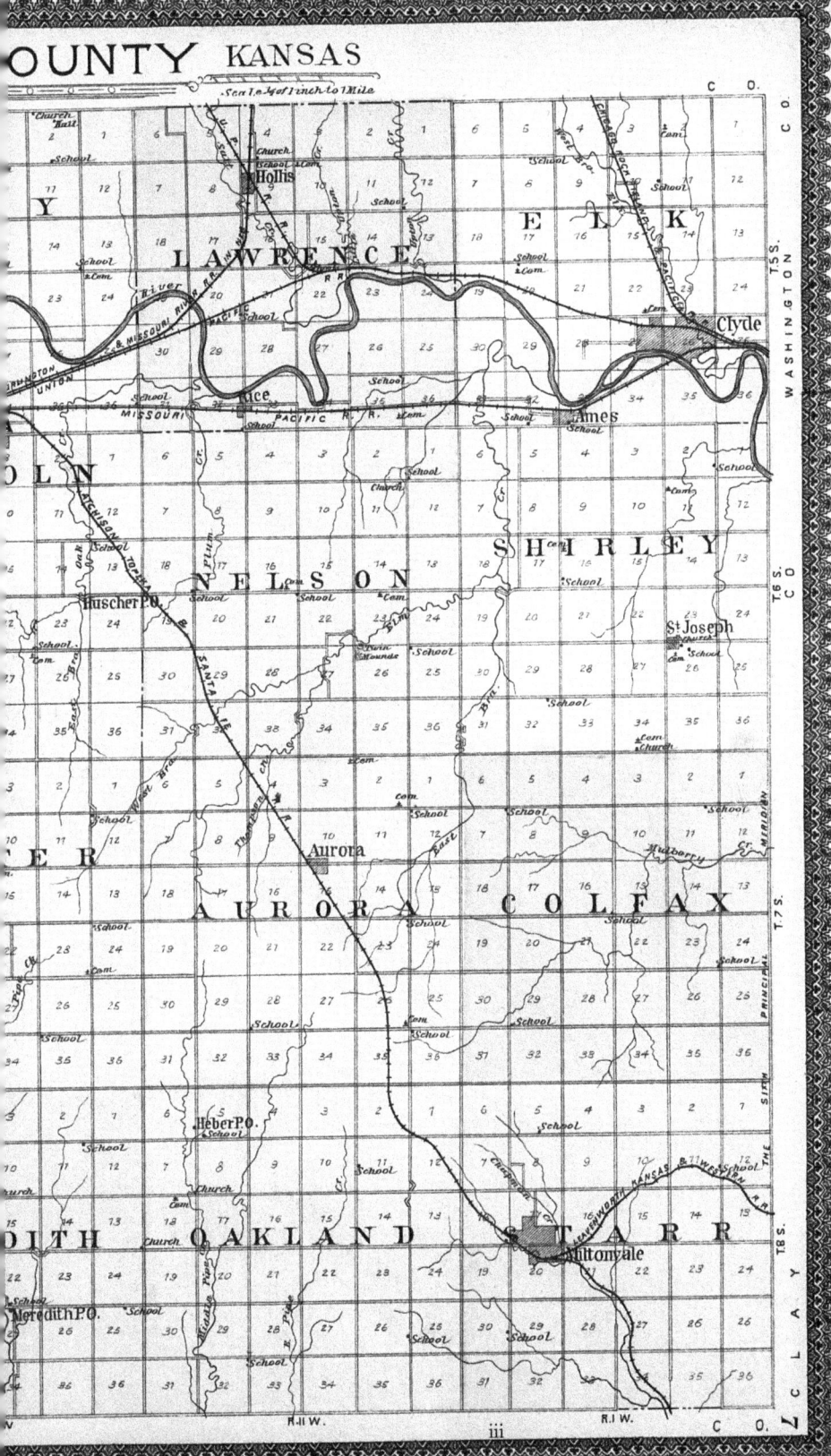

MAP LEGENDS:

Pages ii and iii: 1902 Plat Map, Cloud County, Kansas.

****

Page v: 1902 Plat Map, township of Colfax.
Sections 29 and 32: David & Hiram Woodruff's original homesteads.

****

Pages vi and vii: Map of Clyde.

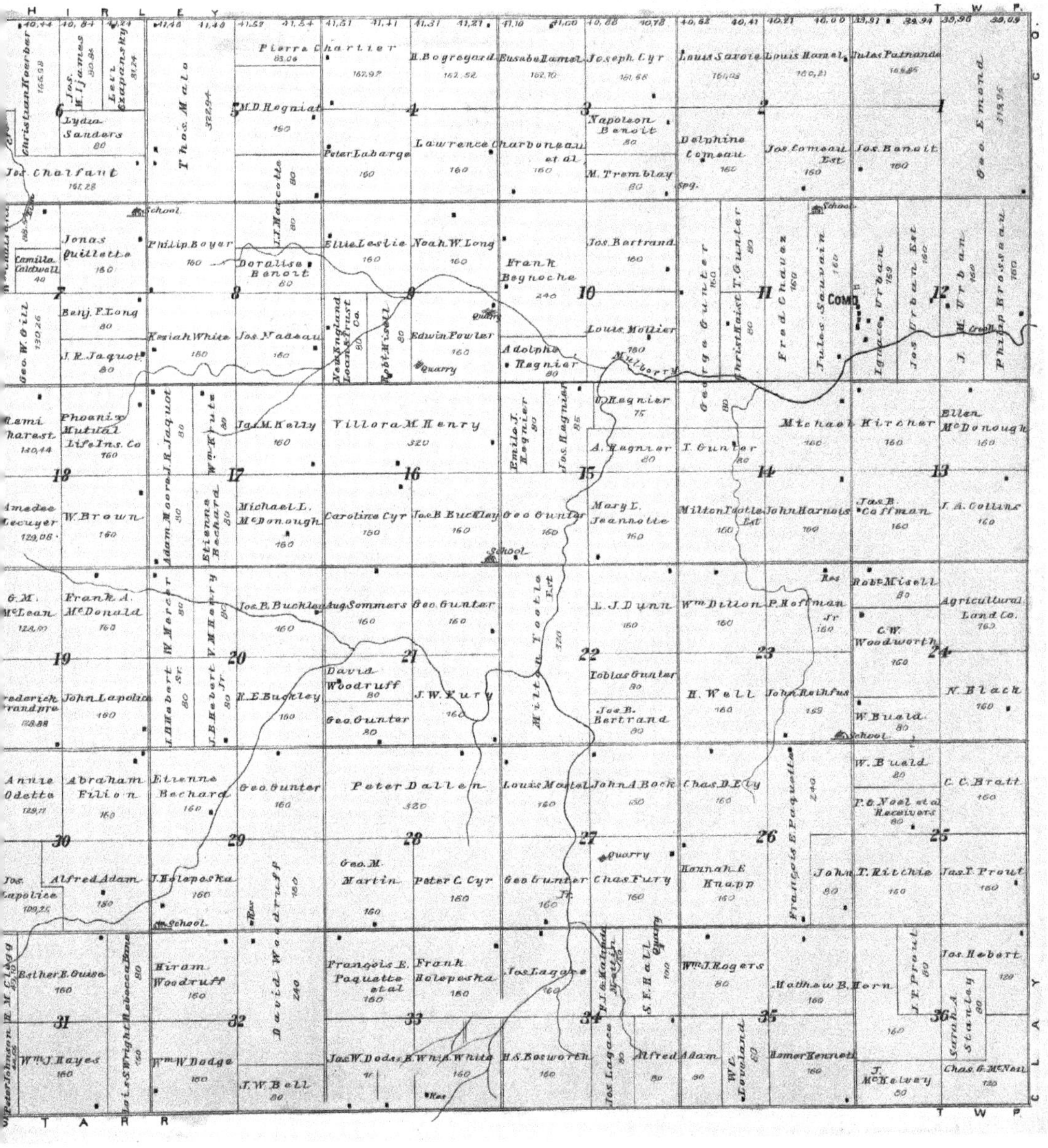

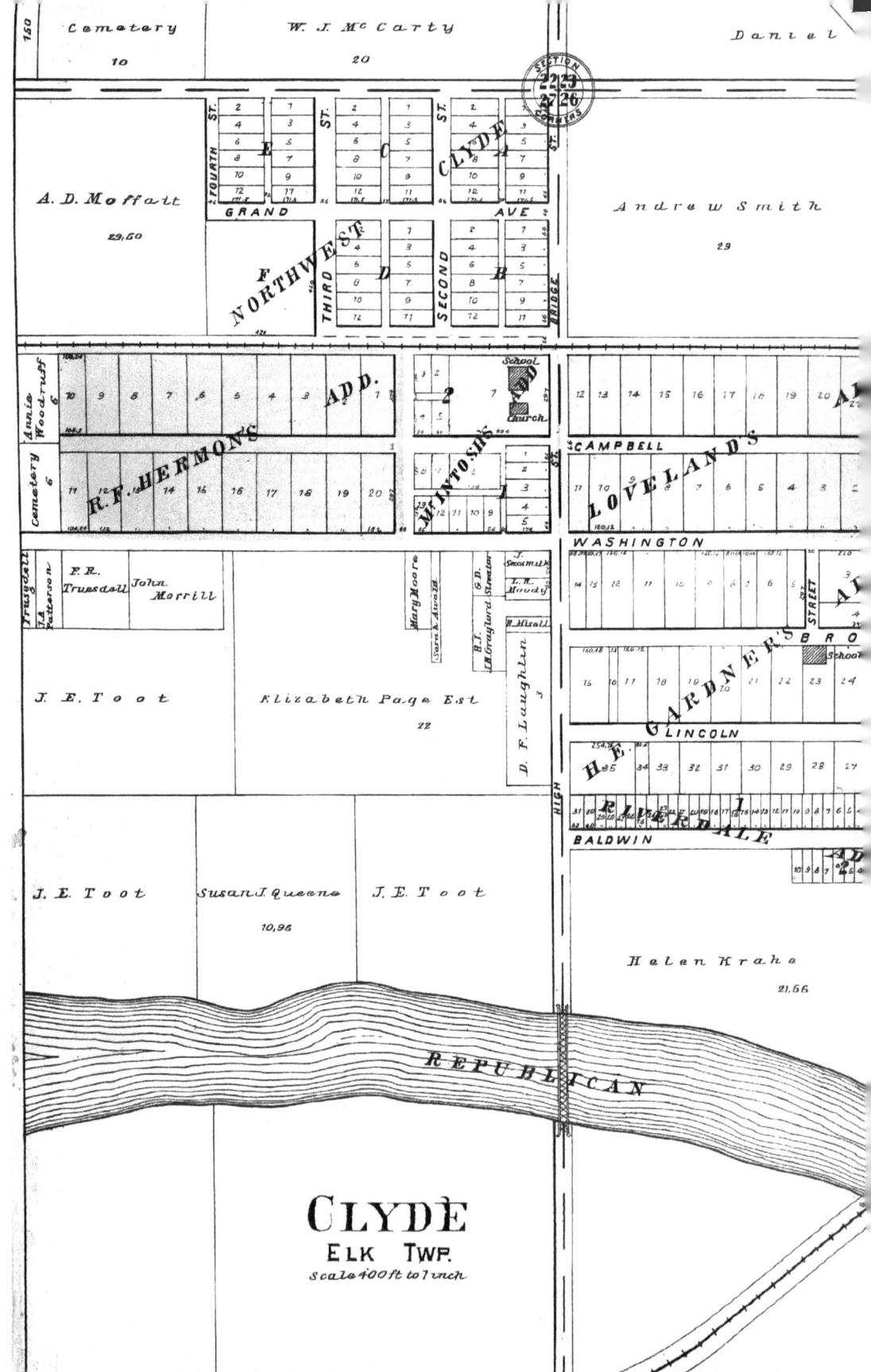

Copyright © 2025 David Hayes.

Edited by: Chris Springer

Cover & Interior Design: Andy Meaden – meadencreative.com

First Printing 2025

ISBN 979-8-9915430-0-2 (Paperback)

ISBN 979-8-9915430-1-9 (eBook)

Disclaimer:

Every effort has been made to portray events in this book as accurately as possible. Every attempt was made to verify the accuracy of all information used. Sources included recorded documents, newspaper articles and family stories. In the case of conflicting data, the most authoritative source has been used. Any errors or omissions are accidental; the author assumes no liability caused by said errors or omissions.

All rights reserved. No portion of this book may be reproduced, stored in a retrieval system, or transmitted in any form or by any means – electronic, mechanical, photocopy, recording, or any other, except for brief quotation in printed reviews, without the prior written permission of the publisher except as provided by USA copyright law.

Title page photo: Isaac Woodruff's children, 1908.
L-R (back row): Ruth, Cesil.
(Center row): Joseph, Timothy, Dorothea, Alma.
(Front): John Alvin.

Contents

Preface	xiii
Introduction	xv
1 Cloud County, Kansas	1
2 The Journey Westward	11
3 1870s: Early Homestead Years	21
4 1880s: Shaping the County	37
5 1890s: Growth and Hardship	49
6 1900s: The Next Generation	63
7 1910s: Zenith	93
8 1920s: Departure	129
Bibliography	135
Appendix A: Woodruff Teachers	139
Appendix B: Woodruff Family Tree	143
Appendix C: Early Woodruff Line	151
Appendix D: Southampton Woodruffs	165
Appendix E: Elizabeth, New Jersey Woodruffs	169
Appendix F: Washington County, Ohio Woodruffs	175
Photographic Credits	179
About the Author	183
Index	185

DEDICATION

*To my loving grandmother, Pauline (Polly) Will,
to whom family was the most important thing of all.*

1898. Ova Woodruff (front row, white dress) at Nelson District School.

Preface

This book chronicles the early years of the Woodruff family in Cloud County, Kansas.

Their story is significant for three reasons. First, the Woodruffs were one of the first families to settle in Cloud County. Second, I have a personal interest in them: my family roots run through the Cloud County Woodruffs. And third, no such research, to my knowledge, has ever been done.

Some 30 years ago, my grandmother, Pauline Will, gave me a binder entitled "Woodruff Family History." It was an old, typewritten manuscript that had obviously been copied and recopied several times. When I asked where she had gotten it from, she merely said, "Oh, from a cousin of mine." What she had given me was the Woodruff family tree, compiled by Abba Lincoln Shepard in the early twentieth century and retyped by Edmond Silas Woodruff, a second-generation resident of Cloud County. In my hands was family history going back 16 generations, to sixteenth-century England.

The early years of this particular Woodruff line have already been extensively researched. Over half a dozen volumes have been published on it. They recount the early days in England; immigration to the colonies; the family's part in the founding of Southampton, Long Island; their role in establishing Elizabeth, New Jersey; the Revolutionary War; and contributions to Washington County, Ohio. These are all well documented in the numerous books. But detailed records for the period after their stay in Washington County, Ohio, could not be found. For the branch that had migrated to Kansas, no information was available except for a handful of photographs and isolated family stories.

For the past four generations, my branch of the family has lived in California. It is well known that our Woodruff line came through Cloud County. My great-grandmother shared her recollections about growing up on the farm in Kansas. When I was 13, I traveled to Aurora with my great-grandfather, who took me to where the farm had been. He told me stories about driving his Model T Ford down the road the farm was on (to this day, it remains a dirt road). I even have a photo of myself standing next to the old barn (which was standing in the 1970s but is now long gone).

Fortunately, my older cousins had taken the time to speak with their parents, preserved photos and mementos, and could recount lore about their families. I extend my sincere thanks to Pam Coon, Paul Huscher, Jay Parker, Evelyn Parsons, and Clayton Walker—and my beloved late grandmother, Polly Will—for sharing their history and memories, making this work possible.

Now, after several hundred hours of painstaking research, I have compiled a much more detailed history of the Cloud County Woodruffs. This is not a scholarly text; it is not even, by any means, complete. Much more can be added, and hopefully, someone will undertake that task in the future. But this text is a start, and I have published it in this form so that what has been discovered so far is not lost.

I want to keep the memories alive. And if this book fills in a missing piece of history for Cloud County, or helps someone discover part of their own family, then I have succeeded.

David G. Hayes

Introduction

This is a story of the real America.

It is the story of how this country was built. It is not a story of presidents or historical figures, nor of famous generals or celebrated battles. Yet the figures in this account were just as important in making the nation what it is today. A country is defined by its people; what they do, think, and feel is the true fabric of any society.

This is a glimpse into the growth of Cloud County, Kansas, and how one family helped to establish and shape it during its early years into what it is today.

Most of these men and women were not famous. Some were noteworthy enough to have earned their places in various historical texts; all were well known and were respected by those who knew them. Through hard work and civic involvement, they molded their towns and defined the country they lived in. Banding together with other like-minded pioneers, they settled an untamed land and established a thriving, vibrant community for the benefit of all. This pattern repeated itself in thousands of locales across the country, which is how our nation came to be.

The Woodruffs were one of the early families to settle in Cloud County. For generations, they could be found from Aurora to

Miltonvale, from Colfax to Clyde, from Huscher to Sulphur Springs. The name Woodruff was as well-known and respected as any in the county at the time. Family members established schools, built bridges, held public offices, and established thriving farms and businesses. They brought melons for the first annual Watermelon Festival in Clyde—a festival that is still being held more than a century later. When the first rural mail routes were established, Woodruffs served the routes in horse-drawn wagons. When the railroads planned new routes, it was a Woodruff who spearheaded the crusade to have the railway run through their town, in the hope that it would bring prosperity with it.

Alongside the triumphs were heartbreaks: floods, accidents, deaths, and more. The region these settlers chose could be harsh and unforgiving. But these were strong, resilient men and women. They endured these misfortunes and heartbreaks, emerging stronger. Theirs is the real story of America. It is about how one family lived, worked, and, in their own way, helped create their community—and a nation.

This is the Woodruff story.

Cloud County near Rice Township, looking south towards Aurora.

1
Cloud County, Kansas

Cloud County, Kansas, sits just south of the Nebraska border. It is only a few miles from Lebanon, Kansas (the geographic center of the United States), putting it, quite literally, at the center of the country.

It is not large; the entire population could even fit onto a large modern cruise ship. As of this writing, the county has roughly the same number of people as it did in the 1870s.

Yet this small county is part of American history. It was part of the great expansion westward and has made its own contributions to the country.

Like all areas of Kansas, Cloud County is almost entirely farmland. Small townships sit like islands among the fields of wheat, corn, oats, and other crops. Some areas display the table-top flatness typical of many other parts of the state. Others, like the southeast region, have low, gentle, rolling hills. In springtime, particularly after a rain, the landscape is covered in a sea of green, which rivals the lush emerald countryside of Ireland. Livestock, primarily cattle and hogs, are common sights along the country roads. Various kinds of wildlife also make their home here. Dozens of different species of birds can be found; raccoons and deer can be spotted along the rivers and near the forests.

Cloud County currently has 18 townships, seven incorporated cities, and five unincorporated communities. Taken together, the entire area boasts just over nine thousand residents, but over five thousand of them are concentrated in the county seat, Concordia. Of the remaining communities, only Clyde can claim more than five hundred citizens. Many of the others, according to the 2020 census, do not even top one hundred people.[1]

Although small in population, the region is rich in hospitality. Concordia has been called the "Friendliest Small Town in the United States," and with good reason. The inhabitants are both courteous and helpful; visitors are welcomed and made to feel like part of the community. This warmth is expressed in the remaining townships as well. Striking up a conversation with a stranger is as comfortable as with a family member. On the roads, residents will, more often than not, smile and wave to anyone passing in the other direction, be it a neighbor or a random traveler.

The reason for this widespread cordiality stems largely from the region itself. In the early pioneering years, the landscape was harsh; the land, while arable, was difficult to cultivate. Weather and natural disasters were constant threats. Drought (or a flood), tornadoes, and plagues such as locusts could wipe out years of hard work. Farming by hand in this era was difficult and exhausting. Settlers were widely scattered; it was not uncommon for the nearest neighbor to be a mile or more away. Contact with others could be rare. "Prairie fever" (or "prairie madness") was a real and serious affliction, caused by

---

[1] This refers to incorporated cities and unincorporated communities. There are three townships that have populations between 600 and 800 residents.

the harsh living conditions and extreme isolation. Those from urban settings or closely knit social environments were particularly susceptible. Its symptoms were akin to extreme depression. In extreme cases, mental breakdowns were not uncommon, which could cause violence, madness, or even suicide.

The pioneers learned to value their neighbors. Life on the plains was demanding, even at the best of times. No settler could survive alone, physically or mentally. Disasters and calamities would sooner or later touch nearly everyone attempting to tame this land. And when they did, the community would band together and help those who had been stricken. It required strength and an independent nature to homestead in the plains. But it also required a tight-knit community, where every individual was valued. Close friends and family could always be counted on for support. Even unfamiliar residents were regarded as friendly rather than as potential threats.

Republican River

Across the northern part of the county runs the Republican River. This waterway has always played a pivotal role in the area, both good and bad. Where there is agriculture, there is a need for water. Some areas were fortunate to have small streams or springs. Many of the crops relied only on rain. Depending too much on precipitation was risky, as the region was prone to droughts. The largest and most dependable source of water was the Republican River. Originating in the High Plains of Colorado, it flows through the northern part of the county, eventually joining the Smoky Hill River and forming the Kansas River some miles southeast. Several townships, including two of the largest, Concordia and Clyde, sit near its banks.

Republican River, just north of Concordia, Kansas.

Early History

Cloud County is part of the Great Plains—that flat, grassy prairie land between the Mississippi River and the Rocky Mountains. In the past, the region was seen as far more inhospitable than it is today. In 1820, Major Stephen Long headed an expedition across the region. The map he published labeled it "The Great American Desert." It was considered undesirable for settlement due to extreme weather conditions and a lack of wood and water sources. The methods used for raising crops at the time made it unfit for farming.[2] In the expedition's report, the party's geographer wrote:

> *I do not hesitate in giving the opinion, that it is almost wholly unfit for cultivation, and of course, uninhabitable by a people depending upon agriculture for their subsistence. Although tracts of fertile land considerably extensive are occasionally to be met with, yet the scarcity of wood and water, almost uniformly prevalent, will prove an insuperable obstacle in the way of settling the country.*

As a result, the region remained sparsely populated for many years. Then, in 1862, came the Homestead Act. By living continuously on a homestead for five years and paying a small filing fee, settlers were able to acquire full ownership of a 160-acre farm. The lure of free land brought hundreds of thousands of people westward to what was then considered bleak, hostile, desolate wastelands. For many, this was the only way they would be able to acquire land; for others, this was the promise of a new and better life.

Shirley Township, established in 1859, was originally part of Washington County. In 1866, the residents sent James Hageman to the state governor with a petition requesting the right to form their own county.[3] The governor approved the request, and Shirley Township became Shirley County.

The county was divided into townships, one of which was Shirley. Clyde, established in 1866, was the oldest city in the county, and as it was the only organized settlement of any size, it became the temporary county seat.

---

2   The fact that Major Long's expedition was conducted during a dry period contributed greatly to the conclusion that the land was desert.

3   James Hageman is credited as the leader of this movement.

James Hageman was active in local political affairs. He was elected county clerk, then ran for the state House of Representatives. In his first campaign, he lost to John B. Rupe of Clyde. A few years later, when Hageman ran again, he (just barely) won a seat, becoming Shirley's first representative to the state legislature.

Hageman's dislike of Clyde might have stemmed from his electoral loss to Rupe. It might have been a dislike of the man himself that was then transferred to the town. Regardless of the reason, frictions increased when Rupe proposed a bill that would partition the new county: half would be given to Ottawa County and the other half to Republic County. Hageman vigorously opposed the bill, and it was defeated. However, his dislike and distrust of Rupe—and Clyde in general—grew even more deep-seated.

Hageman's dislike curdled into animosity when Rupe introduced a proposal to change the county name. Shirley County was originally named for Massachusetts governor William Shirley. However, Rupe incorrectly claimed that it had been named for a notorious prostitute from Fort Riley named Jane Shirley. He stated that the county should be "named for a man of honor rather than a woman of ill fame" and proposed renaming it for Civil War veteran Colonel William Cloud. The proposal was passed, and Shirley County became Cloud County.[4]

Tensions between Hageman and Clyde finally came to a head over a bad business deal. He had approached Clyde officials, offering to purchase an acre of land, on which he intended to live and to build and operate a hotel. The land he selected was offered to him by the city at a reasonable price. But before the transaction could be completed, Clyde changed its offer, substituting a different—and less desirable—acre for a higher price.

At that point, Hageman swore he was finished with all business

---

[4] Ironically, although the county's name was changed to Cloud, Shirley Township's name remained unchanged.

dealings with Clyde and was determined that it would never become the county seat. He took a claim in nearby Lincoln Township and built a home. With his own money, he had a road survey done from Junction City to his residence. And as a member of the state legislature, he had the state build the road. The finished product was a red sandstone highway named "64 Milepost Road," supposedly named for its length.

United States law required that all new counties set aside a quarter section of land (160 acres), divided into lots and sold; the proceeds would be used for the construction of public buildings. Together with G. W. Andrews and William English, Hageman selected Section 33, Township 5, Range 3 west and named it Concordia, after a town of the same name in Missouri. This was platted (divided) into blocks. The men even indicated the spot for the courthouse and a park. The future county seat had been created—but only on paper. The only structure actually in place was Hageman's house.

Hageman circulated a petition asking the board of supervisors to hold an election to choose a permanent county seat. Up until this time, Clyde had been the temporary county seat. The election was held on 21 December 1869. The potential sites were Sibley (now extinct, originally north of the Republic River), Clyde, and Concordia.

Sibley had the most eligible voters of the three and, all other things being equal, would likely have prevailed in the voting. But all other things were not equal. Hageman was accused of allowing non-residents to vote. There were claims that he smuggled liquor to Sibley's polling place to sway votes or get the voting ruled invalid.

Regardless, when the votes were tallied, Concordia prevailed and was proclaimed the official county seat.

The Republic Land District Office, the first official agency to operate within the city limits, opened on 15 January 1871. This brought a flow of settlers into the new city, as they needed to file their homestead claims. Concordia's plat map was filed nearly three months later, on 3 March 1871, officially making Concordia a city.

The Truesdell family wanted to open what would be one of the first hotels in Concordia. Building materials were in short supply, so rather than wait for lumber to be delivered to build a new structure, the Truesdells simply moved their own large house into town. It took 11 yoke of oxen and four men to haul the building over hill, in one piece. And while it was being transported, the Truesdells continued living in it.

A handful of other businesses opened that first year. Many of the retail advertisements in the local paper were for businesses in other cities, such as Clyde, Fort Leavenworth, and St. Louis. Concordia, while officially a city and a county seat, was essentially a handful of wooden structures, lined with dusty dirt roads.

This unlikely place, which had emerged from plans on paper, was where the Woodruff story began.

Isaac Woodruff, on his farm in Aurora, Kansas, 1918.

1870s wagon train crossing the American plain.

2
The Journey Westward

Three Brothers

In the early spring of 1871, a small group of pioneers departed from Watertown, Ohio, and headed west. Traveling together were three brothers: Hiram, David, and Anson Woodruff, sons of Silas Woodruff.

It is not surprising that they embarked upon this journey. Theirs was a true American pioneering family, descendants of the original Woodruff stock who originated in Fordwich, England. Arriving at the Massachusetts colony in 1639, they were among the founders of Southampton, Long Island; then later, Elizabeth, New Jersey; and eventually Marietta and Washington counties in Ohio. In the historical annals of each place, they are listed as a family of prominence. By the 1870s, there had already been four generations of Woodruffs in the Ohio region.

The three brothers' father, Silas Woodruff, was well known and respected. In 1902, the *History of Marietta and Washington County, Ohio*, noted:

Silas Woodruff is a highly esteemed man, and is noted far and wide for his charity and benevolence. He is a man of large means, oil having been discovered on his land, and several wells being in operation there.[5]

Silas had a large and very prosperous farm. In 1870, along with a sizable house, he had 250 acres of farmland valued at $10,000 (nearly $2 million at today's prices). The farm included fields producing Indian corn, cotton, potatoes, sweet potatoes, cane sugar, and wheat. There was a productive orchard; he made molasses from the cane sugar; his dairy cattle provided not only milk but also hundreds of pounds of butter per year.

Hiram Woodruff

Born on 17 October 1835, Hiram was Silas's second son. A veteran of the Civil War, he served in the 148th Regiment, Ohio Infantry (National Guard), from 17 May 1864 to 14 September 1864.

For many years, he had been a successful farmer in Watertown, Ohio; in 1870 he had an 80-acre farm whose land alone was valued at $2,500 (over $500,000 at today's prices). He kept 65 head of livestock, counting horses, cows, oxen, sheep, and pigs. As was common at the time, he raised crops of rye, Indian corn, and oats. However, unlike most farmers in the region, he did not grow wheat.

At the outset of the journey, Hiram was 47 years old. It was unusual for someone to begin such an arduous journey at such a late age, especially if that person was also a prosperous farmer. The three brothers' father, Silas, had remarried in 1859 and now had three additional young sons to provide for, along with another daughter. Hiram's existing farm had less than 40 acres prepared for planting; his family had six children, most of whom were too young

---

[5] M. R. Andrews, *History of Marietta and Washington County, Ohio* (Chicago: Biographical Publishing Company, 1902), vol. 2, 242.

to contribute effectively to running the farm. The promised 160 acres would double his land holdings.

These two factors—father Silas's remarriage and the opportunity to expand the family land holdings—were likely what motivated Hiram's decision to head westward.

Hiram headed west in the early spring of 1871, in a simple wagon pulled by a span of mules. Traveling with him was his wife, Sarah Amanda (née Gilmore), and their six children. (Their two youngest at the time—twins Anna and Margaret—had died the year before, aged only two days old.) Sarah was a tough, red-headed Welsh woman with a stern disposition. She was also four months pregnant with their ninth child, Clark, when they set out. Their children traveling west with them were:

- Della, 13 years old (b. 16 July 1858)
- Florence, 11 years old (b. 9 March 1860)
- Isaac, 9 years old (b. 17 January 1862)
- Cora, 7 years old (b. 23 February 1864)
- Albert, 6 years old (b. 20 December 1865)
- Lewis, 3 years old (b. 30 March 1868)

Four more children were born after the family arrived at their new Kansas home:

- Clark (b. 18 September 1871, just a month or two after arriving in Kansas)
- Jessie (b. 16 March 1874)
- Livinia ("Linnie") (b. 21 September 1876)
- Dora (b. 13 June 1879)

Sarah Amanda Gilmore, 1858.

After establishing himself in Kansas, Hiram was somewhat active in local affairs but for the most part stayed out of the spotlight and concentrated on farming. He was widely recognized as one of the more hard-working and productive farmers in the region.

David Woodruff

David Woodruff was well-regarded and respected by the citizens of Cloud County. He was considered kind, honest, and good-hearted. A prominent figure, he was consistently praised in the newspapers as intelligent, thrifty, ambitious, and of impeccable character.

In Barlow, Ohio, he lived with his father, Silas, until the age of 17, when he left home and became a teacher. Near the end of the Civil War, he enlisted in Company I, 148th Ohio Volunteers. After the conflict was over, he returned home, again living with his parents, and resumed his schoolhouse duties.

One source states that David moved from Barlow Township, Ohio, to Cloud County, Kansas, in 1905.[6] However, newspaper and other accounts indicate that he was already in Cloud County as early as 1871 and already active in public affairs.

He married his cousin and childhood sweetheart, Victoria Browning, in Ohio before embarking west. Many members of the Browning family lived in Cloud County in the years after the 1871 journey, so it is likely that they and the Woodruffs traveled together.

David and Victoria had seven children:

- Carl Woodruff (b. 12 April 1873)
- Lulu May (June) Woodruff (b. 11 August 1874)
- Arthur Clyde Woodruff (b. 28 May 1877)

---

6   C. Woodruff and M. R. Herod, *Woodruff Chronicles, a Genealogy*, vol. 2 (Glendale: Arthur H. Clark Company, 1971).

- Edmond Silas Woodruff (b. 15 September 1878)
- Emmette Woodruff (b. 4 August 1882)
- Ethel Leona Woodruff (b. 9 October 1884)
- Pearl Lena Woodruff (b. 18 March 1891)

Like his older brother Hiram, David became a prosperous farmer in the area. But he took a much more active role in local affairs. He taught, established a school, and held public offices in Colfax Township for years, most notably as Colfax town trustee and judge. He was nominated and ran for several other county offices and at one point was considered as a potential state senator by citizens in the southeast portion of the county. Several newspapers endorsed the idea. As township trustee, he was responsible for the care of the poor and those in need of assistance. He was also directly involved in many other activities that benefited the local towns and county, such as building bridges, and was instrumental in efforts to get the railroad to run a line through the southeast region of the county, including Colfax Township.

Anson Woodruff

Anson Woodruff was the youngest of the three brothers who came to and eventually settled in Cloud County. Compared to his brothers, he was less of a farmer and more of an adventurer. He was fond of hunting and trapping; there are several confirmed accounts of him taking hunting trips, often for weeks or months. He frequently ventured north to Nebraska, sometimes returning with several hundred pelts. He would fish in the local streams and occasionally sell his catch in town. At times he owned farmland in Cloud County but more often made his home in town.

Little is known about his early life. He was a Civil War veteran; on 17 March 1864, at age 16, he enlisted in the 36th Regiment,

Company F, Ohio, and served as a drummer. After the war, he continued playing the drum, founding the Woodruff Drum Corps and performing for public events. His sons were also active in the corps.

After leaving Ohio in 1871, he stopped for one year in Independence, Missouri, before joining his brothers in Cloud County. It is presumed that he got to Independence by traveling with his brothers, as the town is along the routes of the wagon trail that they most likely used.

Like Hiram and David, he held public offices but was never a major public figure. Within the first two years of arriving in Cloud County, he became town constable and occasionally served as an election official. He might have risen to greater prominence in the community had it not been for a scandal that marred his public career early on. As a constable, he took a business trip to a nearby county, accompanied by a cousin, Frank Browning, and the two were involved in an incident in which Browning died. While not at fault, Anson was briefly jailed by the local sheriff until the judge eventually dropped the charges. But as the incident involved excessive drinking, and Cloud County was a dry county until 1990, this likely dashed any hopes of more prominent public involvement.

After residing for several years in Cloud County, Anson married Anna Jane Neill. The couple had eight children:

- James Anson Woodruff (b. 5 February 1878)
- William Woodruff (b. 16 March 1879)
- Silas Woodruff (b. 12 February 1882)
- Annie May Woodruff (b. 16 July 1884)
- Charles Scott Woodruff (b. 3 January 1888)
- Bennie Woodruff (b. 17 April 1890)
- Lena Joanna Woodruff (b. 19 December 1892)

- Fannie Mariah Woodruff (b. 9 February 1895)

The couple might also have had a ninth child, born circa January 1891; no birth record can be found, but local newspapers reported the death of "the Woodruff's infant boy" in Clyde in March 1891.[7]

In later years, Anson became one of the first three carriers appointed for the newly created Rural Free Delivery routes. He retired shortly afterwards, handing the position to his nephew Edmond Silas Woodruff.

For over two hundred years before 1871, Woodruffs had repeatedly traveled to wild, unexplored lands. There, they tamed the land and, together with other like-minded individuals, built towns and communities, quietly making their mark in history.

Now the three brothers were leaving their home in Ohio to do this once again, this time in Cloud County, Kansas.

---

[7] I. C. Ewe, "Dry Creek Items," *Clyde Argus*, Clyde, Kansas, 20 March 1891, page 5, column 5.

Concordia, 1872

3
1870s: Early Homestead Years

The 1870s were an eventful decade for America. The 15th Amendment was passed. The Chicago Fire raged for days, killing hundreds and leaving hundreds of thousands homeless. The Reconstruction Era officially ended. Thomas Edison invented the first commercially viable light bulb. Morgan silver dollars were first minted. The National League of Baseball was founded.

The Wild West was still very much alive. General George Custer was killed in the Battle of Little Bighorn. In 1871, Wild Bill Hickok served as marshal, first in Hays City, then in Abilene, Kansas—just a day's ride away from Cloud County by stagecoach. Five years later, he was killed playing poker in Deadwood, South Dakota.

Starr Township's first settler, William Zahn, constructed a massive 23-by-40-foot stone house (complete with two stories and a basement) to replace his original dugout home. This became the "halfway house" for settlers en route to Clay Center or Junction City.

This is the Kansas that welcomed David and Hiram Woodruff when they arrived in Cloud County.

In the 1870s, the incoming tide of settlers began to change the area from empty prairie into a region dotted with farms and homesteads. The county's population (according to the US census) jumped from zero in 1860 to 2,323 in 1870, with more continuing to arrive from the east. Cloud County was still in its infancy. The county seat, Concordia, had been formally established in 1870 but didn't actually exist until a year later. Apart from Clyde, the county had no real towns or cities.

It took the Woodruffs at least four months to complete their arduous 900-mile journey from Ohio to Kansas. Though they were traveling during the best time of year, they averaged only about seven-and-a-half miles per day. They homesteaded in what eventually became the township of Colfax. This flat, barren land was vastly different from their old home in Washington County, Ohio. There they had been on rich, fertile farmland.

The Woodruffs' new Kansas home in the "Great American Desert" had only one tree—a cottonwood—in the entire countryside around them. The nearest village was Waterville,[8] which was 56 miles away—a two-day ride. Their home was a simple hut made of sod, the only building material available. They would hitch their mules to the old wagon and gather the buffalo chips found all over the prairie—the only available fuel to use for their cooking and heating.

For the first year, they existed on what vegetables and Indian corn they could grow by chopping holes in the sod, which had to

---

8 Probably in Smith County.

be turned over with an axe or spade. David and Hiram, who had adjacent homesteads, joined farms, often working together.

Fortunately, Major Long and his party were wrong when they reported the area unfit for cultivation. While it was unproductive using the methods employed at the time, it was not poor land. In fact, William G. Cutler wrote:

> *The soil of the valleys is exceedingly rich and friable—a rich alluvial, from three to ten feet in depth. The uplands consist of a black vegetable mould, ranging from ten inches to three feet in depth. In favorable seasons the uplands yield very large crops.... Like the soil of Nebraska, it is most admirably constituted to stand both drouth [sic] and wet seasons, it being very porous to a great depth.*[9]

The county was not blessed with much surface water; many wells had to be dug, sometimes as deep as 100 feet down. The Woodruffs wisely chose an area with both rich soil and available water. Mulberry Creek, the main tributary through Colfax Township, provided a year-round supply. This allowed them to fully tap the potential of their homestead. The new farming methods had changed greatly from the old ways, as David Woodruff described after a trip to visit his father's farm in Ohio:

> *They still cling to the old mode of farming back there. They use about 3 bu. of fertilizing to the acre for small grain. They check their corn, ground with a single shovel blow. One man drops the corn in the hill, another follows and drops a spoonful of fertilizing in each hill, another follows and covers with a hoe.*[10]

---

9 W. G. Cutler, *History of the State of Kansas* (Chicago: A. T. Andreas, 1883), p. 1014.
10 *Clyde Voice-Republican*, 26 June 1902, page 2, column 6.

Until 1870, only a handful of townships had been formed. When Cloud County was created in 1866, the only established town was Clyde. Over the next four years, several others came into existence, including Glasco, Jamestown, Minersville,[11] and the county seat, Concordia.

Colfax Township was incorporated on 11 April 1872, with W. F. Campbell as the first trustee. As they had homesteaded the previous year, both Hiram and David Woodruff were counted among the first citizens in Colfax Township.

The population density by now was roughly three persons (one family) per square mile. The influx of homesteaders into Cloud County continued; it was starting to become a thriving agricultural region. By 1873, the population had doubled; so had the acreage planted for crops. Anson Woodruff left Independence, Missouri, and joined his brothers Hiram and David in Aurora/Colfax.

Eighteen seventy-four was an eventful year. All three brothers became active in civic affairs, especially ambitious and energetic David. He was appointed Colfax trustee—a position he would hold for the next 13 years. Anson Woodruff was appointed constable. All three—Hiram, David, and Anson—were regular clerks and judges for local elections over the next several years.

David shouldered additional public and social responsibilities. On top of tending his farm and acting as township trustee, he served the community through various beneficial organizations. In 1875, he was appointed vice president of the Cloud County Aid Society in Colfax, which purchased and distributed relief supplies to the county's destitute—including seeds for planting (much had been lost the previous year to the locusts). He was director of the Cloud County Agricultural and Mechanical Association, which, among other things, was involved in establishing and holding the county fair.

---

11 Created in 1869, after coal was discovered. The population peaked at 500 and consisted mostly of miners living in dugouts.

This workload would have been taxing enough for most men. But David Woodruff apparently possessed inexhaustible energy, for he took on even more responsibilities. In 1875 he was elected justice of Colfax; in 1876 he was also county assessor.

Township Officers.

The following is a list of the township officers elected in the various townships of Cloud county on Tuesday, Nov. 5, 1878.

TOWNSHIPS.	TRUSTEES.	CLERKS.	TREASURERS.	JUSTICES.	CONSTABLES.
Elk,	John B. Rupe,	L. H. Sayre,	P. McDonald,		Baker Borton, R. V. Vining.
Lawrence,	W. H. Morgan,	I. R. Davis,	L. D. Lawrence,		John Spear, W. H. Brower
Sibley,	C. D. Avery,	G. Parker,	C. V. Miller,		F. A. Stilson, T. Donoley.
Buffalo,	J. F. Hannum,	W. C. Williams,	T. Ramsey,		Jno. Glidden, L. J. White.
Grant,	H. F. Burdick,	Henry Gray,	Wm. J. Ion,	H. Andrews,	C. Cutshaw, I. Lockard.
Summit,	Sidney Brown,	J. C. Orput,	Jno. Riddell,		E. L. Reece, A. W. Burcher
Arion,	Nathan Doak,	A. Nelson,	A. R. Maddox,		E. Jennings, Jno. Spiker.
Lincoln,	E. L. Prince,	H. Byrne,	C. F. Hostetler,	Jas. Hagaman, A. A. Carnahan.	J. A. Linton, Al. Pennock.
Center,	Jno. Myers,	A. Whitehead,	W. H. Ritchey	J. F. Fish, W. F. Compton	Sol. Peiffer, George Scott.
Nelson,	H. H. Young,	A. L. Thomas,	H. B. Parvin,		F. P. Allen, Lyman Rice.
Shirley.	F. Chavey,	L. B. Wilcox,	F. L. Coron.	D. B. Dutton, F. Breausau.	L. O. Fuller, R. T. Cardinal.
Colfax,	D. Woodruff,	W. Campbell,	H. J. Varney,		John Bruce, H. J. Varney.
Starr,	O. Loomis,	Jno. H. Miller,	J W. Matthews,	G. T. Mock, R. S. Phelps.	W. H. Mock, Wm. Adams.
Aurora,	F. A. Thompson,	A. G. Smith.	E. R. Jones,		L. Archambos, G. W. Ring.
Oakland,	Ed. Marshall,	G. M. Kreger,	Jas. Connolley,		J. H. Moger, S. E. Smith.
Meredith,	T. S. Rolph,	J. R. Hogg,	G. W. Carver,	B. F. Ord, T. Tisdell.	Jno. Breen, L. J. Carver.
Lyon,	W. H. Ward,	M. W. Webster,	H. A. Newell,	W. Woodward, E. Bainum.	J. M. Hore, W. E. Caldwell.
Solomon,	Jacob Studt,	J. M. Copeland,	Wm. Butler,		J. P. Thompson F. Chapman.

David Woodruff elected Township Trustee, Colfax Township, 1878.

He did not neglect his previous occupation as teacher. He taught school and established a schoolhouse in 1872 (District 61). For decades to come, this was known as the "Woodruff Schoolhouse"; it hosted the first Sunday school class for Colfax/Sulphur Springs in 1877. He assisted the Teachers' Institute for Cloud County, contributing to the annual programs and examinations.

David was without question a driving force in establishing Colfax during its formative years. He ran his farm, held three public offices, served as an executive of two charitable organizations, and raised a family simultaneously. It is doubtful that there was any more influential figure in the township at that time.

In 1870, there had been an extreme dry period; the region saw a summer where 42 days passed without rain, and some of the crops failed as a result. Over the next couple years, several more dry spells hit the area, though they were not as severe. The legislature passed appropriations to relieve drought sufferers. And despite the low precipitation, these were good crop years.

Unfortunately for the farmers, the drought intensified.

The year 1874 saw the longest dry spell in memory. Only 18 inches of rain fell in as many months—half the normal amount. During the hottest part of the year, two months passed with literally no rain at all. The Reverend W. Bristow, pastor of a church in Eureka, Kansas, reported:

> *The 14th day of June a heavy rain fell; all through the months of July and August occasionally heavy black clouds would loom up in the west, but no rain would come; the wheat crop was cut short; the chinch bugs went from the wheat fields into the corn fields; then came the hot winds like a blast furnace until it seemed that nothing green could survive.*[12]

Then came the Great Grasshopper Plague of 1874.

---

12 Frank W. Blackmar, ed., *Kansas: A Cyclopedia Of State History, Embracing Events, Institutions, Industries, Counties, Cities, Towns, Prominent Persons, etc.*, vol. 1 (Chicago: Standard Publishing Company, 1912). Quoted in KSGenWeb, https://www.ksgenweb.org/archives/1912/d/droughts.html.

The grasshoppers (commonly called "Rocky Mountain locusts") were last seen in Kansas some six years earlier, in 1868. This time they devastated nearly every part of the Great Plains. One report described the calamity:

> *The invasion began in late July when without warning millions of grasshoppers, or Rocky Mountain locusts, descended on the prairies from the Dakotas to Texas. The insects arrived in swarms so large they blocked out the sun and sounded like a rainstorm. They ate crops out of the ground, as well as the wool from live sheep and clothing off people's backs. Paper, tree bark, and even wooden tool handles were devoured. Hoppers were reported to have been several inches deep on the ground and locomotives could not get traction because the insects made the rails too slippery.*[13]

The governor called a special session of the state legislature, which approved $73,000 in bonds to help the stricken farmers. The rest of the nation also responded with aid, sending money and supplies, which were often hauled free of charge by the railroads.

Despite the droughts and pestilence, the two older brothers' efforts at farming in their first years in Cloud County yielded impressive results. They had overcome adversity that had defeated many others and transformed their barren acres into two of the most productive farms in the region. Hiram's homestead was doing better than the farm he had worked back in Ohio. An excerpt from the local paper dated 11 October 1878 stated:

---

13 Kansas State Historical Society, "Grasshopper Plague of 1874," June 2003, modified 2016, https://www.kshs.org/kansapedia/grasshopper-plague-of-1874/12070.

Mr. D. Woodruff is another model farmer in Colfax. He has a splendid farm on Mulberry near the south line of the township. Mr. Woodruff is Trustee of the township and the people are all pleased to tell you so, for in him they have an officer that they may be proud of. Mr. W. is one of those neat, careful farmers that know what they are doing. Coming to Kansas seven years ago from Washington, Ohio, without any great amount of this world's goods, he has by indefatigable energy opened up a farm that is pleasant to look upon. He has 75 acres under cultivation, and this year has raised 30 acres of the best corn he has raised since he has been here. He had 7 acres of wheat that went over 25 bushels to the acre, machine measure. Mr. W. built his own house, his stables, granaries, corn cribs, corrals, &c., himself, and has 25 head of cattle, 60 head of hogs, horses, farming implements, and all the necessary machinery to carry on farming successfully.

Near him lives a brother, Mr. Hiram Woodruff, another successful farmer.... Mr. W. has a farm of 160 acres of land—50 acres under cultivation, 25 acres of as good corn as ever was raised in Kansas; and is putting out 14 acres of fall wheat. He has 9 head of cattle and 36 head of hogs. He has a beautiful grove around his house, and all made by his own industry within the last [few] years...[14]

In the summer of 1879, David and Hiram's homestead applications were officially approved. Eight years after their first arrival, they were registered landowners in Cloud County.

---

14 "Gleanings from the Wayside," *Concordia Empire*, Concordia, Kansas, 11 October 1878, page 4, column 3.

Modern view of Hiram Woodruff's original homestead, looking eastward. David Woodruff's homestead is beyond the trees to the left in the background.

The United States of America, To all to whom these presents shall come Homestead Certificate No. 6949 — Greeting.

Application 1327 — Whereas There has been deposited in the General Land Office of the United States a Certificate of the Register of the Land Office at Concordia Kansas, whereby it appears That pursuant to the Act of Congress approved 20th May 1862, "To secure Homesteads to actual Settlers on the Public Domain," and the acts supplemental thereto the claim of Hiram Woodruff has been established and duly consummated in conformity to law for the north-west quarter of section thirty two in township seven south of range one west in the district of lands subject to sale at Concordia Kansas Containing one hundred and sixty acres according to the Official Plat of the Survey of the said Land, returned to the General Land office by the Surveyor General

Now Know ye That there is, therefore, granted by the United States unto the said Hiram Woodruff the tract of Land above described: To have and to hold the said tract of Land with the appurtenances thereof, unto the said Hiram Woodruff and to his heirs and assigns forever.

In testimony whereof, I Rutherford B. Hayes President of the United States of America have caused these letters to be made Patent and the Seal of the General Land Office to be hereunto affixed

Given under my hand at the City of Washington the first day of March in the year of our Lord one thousand eight hundred and seventy nine, and of the Independence of the United States the one hundred and third.

By the President R. B. Hayes By M. M. Sh--- Secretary
Recorded Vol 14 Page 390. S. W. Clark
Recorder of the General Land Office

Entered in transfer record in my office this 23d day of Aug A.D. 1879. D. D. Swearingin County Clerk.
State of Kansas Cloud County ss.
This Instrument was filed for record on the 23d day of Aug A.D. 1879 at 9 o'clock A.M. and duly recorded in Vol J at page 129
C. W. Whipple
Register of Deeds.

Homestead Certificate, Hiram Woodruff, Recorded 23 Aug 1879.
Application No. 1327, Certificate No. 6949.

1870s: EARLY HOMESTEAD YEARS

Homestead Certificate, David Woodruff. Recorded 7 Jul 1879, Application No. 1325, Certificate No. 6980.

Anson Woodruff

Unlike his brothers, young Anson Woodruff was not an industrious farmer; by nature, he was more of an adventurer. As noted previously, he began his new life active in civic affairs and might have pursued a successful career in that direction had it not been for a fateful incident in April 1877.

While Anson was serving as constable for Colfax Township, he and his cousin, Frank Browning,[15] went to Clay Center[16] on business, where they purchased $128 of money orders. While in town, they stayed to patronize the saloons, according to newspaper accounts, "[at] a lively rate all Wednesday afternoon." Unsurprisingly, both became exceedingly drunk. The city marshal put the men in their wagon to send them home; Anson took the reins, while Browning slept in the back. An hour later, they were found by the marshal again, still on the city streets, drunk and unconscious. Anson was roused and started towards Colfax again. Anson wrapped the reins around his wrist and lay down to sleep, giving the horses their lead.

The next morning, the two men were found a few miles away on the roadside, still in their wagon. Anson was fast asleep, but Browning, in the back, was dead.

The body was brought back to Clay Center and placed in the local jail, while a coroner was summoned and a jury convened. The jury deliberated far into the night without coming to a verdict, so they adjourned until the next day.

The following day, Browning's body was missing. It was believed that his friends (and possibly family) had received word of his death, broken into the jail, and retrieved his remains in order to give them

---

15 Brother of Victoria Browning, who was the wife of David Woodruff.
16 County seat of Clay County, 20 miles east of Colfax.

a proper burial.[17] The eventual coroner's verdict was death caused by paralysis of the heart, produced by an overdose of stimulants.

The Clay paper said Frank Browning was "a respectable young man, of excellent business habits, as a general thing, and was not addicted to excessive drinking. His family is one of the most respectable in Washington County, Ohio, from whence he came west to grow up with the country."[18]

Anson was arrested and jailed by the marshal on a complaint by the coroner, charging him with larceny of the clothes covering the corpse. This warrant was issued on the basis of English common law, which held that the clothes covering a corpse were the property of the decedent's estate. The judge who heard the case ruled that Anson could not be held under the statutes of Kansas, and he was released.[19]

However, this was a definite blow to his reputation and character. While he still occasionally served as a local official (assessor, mail carrier, etc.), he never rose above positions of minor authority.

One of the few bright spots for Anson that year was that on 17 April 1877, just a week after his incarceration, he married Anna J. Neill.

Like their farms, the brothers' families grew. After Clark (born shortly after the brothers' arrival in 1871), Hiram added three more to his family: Jessie (1874), Linnie (1876), and Dora (1879). David had four children: Carl (1873), Lulu May "June" (1874), Arthur (1877), and

---

17 Newspaper accounts differ on this point. The general opinion is that Anson himself removed his cousin's body for burial. That is more likely, as the family would not have had enough time to be notified and to travel to do this.
18 "Whiskied to Death," *Concordia Empire*, Concordia, Kansas, 13 April 1877, page 2, column 4.
19 Brother David Woodruff was administrator for the probate of Frank Browning's estate.

Edmond Silas (1878). Even Anson welcomed two children: James (1878) and William (1879).

Hiram's oldest children were now adults and starting their own families. His eldest daughter, Della, married Joseph Campbell on 28 November 1877; their first child, Walter, was born shortly afterwards, on 6 October 1878.

The rail companies made inroads into the county. Five different lines established themselves, crisscrossing the area. Union Pacific was first, connecting Concordia to Kansas City, offering both passenger and mail service. Clyde and Jamestown were stops along the way. The Burlington and Missouri, Santa Fe, and Missouri Pacific also ran through Concordia. Other townships (such as Aurora, Glasco, Huscher, and Miltonvale) gained stations and benefited greatly. Western Union established telegraph service for Concordia in 1878.

As a whole, the county was thriving. The local economy was generating an estimated half a million dollars' worth of business each year—an astounding amount at that time. With a growing economy and population, and the means to transport people, goods, and services, the area was about to come into its own.

The Woodruffs played a sizeable role in this prosperity. Arriving with nothing but the contents of a wagon to build a new home in an empty, flat, treeless land, they had, in less than a decade, overcome drought, plague, and pestilence to establish themselves as hardworking industrious farmers—in fact, among the most successful in the region. They had risen to varying degrees of prominence in public duties, social affairs, and community improvement. As Colfax and other townships continued to expand, so did the effects of the Woodruffs' contributions.

1870s: EARLY HOMESTEAD YEARS

Other locales nearby were also growing. Soon the family would leave their mark on them as well.

1921. Dorothy Johnson, granddaughter of Isaac Woodruff.

Concordia, 1885.

4
1880s: Shaping the County

The United States was flourishing; its population now exceeded 50 million. James A. Garfield was elected president and then, after only 199 days in office, was assassinated by a deranged gunman. The construction of the Washington Monument was completed. Doc Holliday and Virgil and Wyatt Earp had their famous shootout at the OK Corral in Tombstone, Arizona. Jesse James was shot and killed. Buffalo Bill's "Wild West Show" was founded, showcasing Sitting Bull, Calamity Jane, and Annie Oakley.

Like the nation, Cloud County prospered. Concordia was booming; it was now the largest city in the county, twice the size of its rival, Clyde. It boasted 52 retail businesses, one bank, three hotels, nine boarding houses, and two restaurants. The manufacture of local goods increased; there were local makers of flour, brooms, cigars, plows, and washing machines. Over fifteen thousand people now lived in the county—a sevenfold increase in only 10 years.

With the addition of a railroad station in 1882, Milton Tootle's Miltonvale was born.[20] From a small settlement of scattered farms, it grew into a city in 1883, complete with four grocery stores, a bank, and a local newspaper. Four carpenters, a painter, and a plasterer had already set up shop in town. That same year, the city was devastated by fire (the first of many) but was rebuilt.

Despite these advances, the area was not completely tamed. Boston Corbett, the purported killer of Lincoln's assassin, John Wilkes Booth, came to live in Cloud County at this time and stayed until January 1887, when he moved to Topeka and was appointed assistant doorkeeper of the Kansas House of Representatives. One month later, he "adjourned" the assembly at gunpoint, chasing the officers out of the building with a revolver. The following day, he was declared insane and committed to an asylum.

It was no longer the wild, wild West. But nor was it completely civilized like the Eastern regions. David Woodruff's son Edmond recalled what it was like in the 1880s:

> *There were no towns nearer than 16 miles at that time, except a village, called Clyde.*[21]

Each of these townships put its own interests above all else. Rivalries and competitions arose among them; partisan politics was the order of the day. A candidate would often get votes based not only on his party affiliation but also on which township he lived in.

The Woodruff brothers continued running their "model" farms in the southeast corner of the county. While Hiram was still content to

---

20 His original idea for the name was "Tootletown," but the inhabitants wisely chose the proposed "Miltonvale" as a compromise.

21 A. L. Sheppard, *Woodruff Family History* (n.d.) Notes by Edmond Silas Woodruff.

focus on his land, David extended his energies to the organization, expansion, and well-being of Colfax Township and the county as a whole.

Hiram Woodruff

For the most part, Hiram remained outside of public life during these years. He found time to occasionally serve as juror, as well as clerk and treasurer for one of the local schools, but he mainly concentrated his efforts on his farm and family.

Hiram Woodruff and family circa 1890s.
L-R: Linnie, Hiram, wife Sarah Amanda, Dora, Della, Clark.

With his growing prosperity, Hiram built a new house at the same time as his brother David did. While not described in the same glowing terms as David's, it was still considered a fine home.

On 7 April 1886, he welcomed his second grandchild, Nellie Campbell, born to Della (Woodruff) Campbell. In October 1888, his son Albert E. Woodruff married Carrie Huscher. The Huschers were another prominent family in the region. One year before this wedding, the town of Huscher (named after the family) became a shipping point of some importance. The Atchison, Topeka, and Santa Fe Railway had built a branch line from Neva through Huscher to Superior, Nebraska. The year after the wedding, Ada Maude was born (4 May 1889).

On 19 August 1887, Hiram's eldest son, Isaac, married Mary Elizabeth Jennings, a young schoolteacher at one of the rural district schools. Mary was the eldest daughter of Civil War veteran Joshua Jennings (b. 18 June 1837), a handsome man with red whiskers. She had three younger sisters: Nellie and the twins, Alice and Annie. Mary's mother, Electa Van Order, died while giving birth to the twins; Joshua then married the family's servant girl, Sarah Heusted. Together, the new couple produced nine more children of their own. According to family lore, Sarah treated her stepdaughters horribly. While she and her children ate proper meals in the regular dining room, she forced Mary and her sisters to eat in the kitchen, giving them only mush and milk.

After marrying Isaac, Mary continued to teach school, even after the birth of their first child, Ova, on 17 September 1888.

Ova Woodruff ca. 1891.

Isaac's brother Lewis married Mary's sister, Alice Jennings, two years later, on 4 February 1889.

Lewis Woodruff 1887.

David Woodruff

David continued to take a leading role in public affairs. He continued to serve as Colfax trustee; in 1880 he was appointed commissioner to build a bridge over Mulberry Creek, at the south end of Colfax. Subsequent years saw him accepting positions as commissioner for various projects, township assessor, delegate to the Concordia Republican convention and the county central committee, judge and clerk of elections, and chairman of the county board of supervisors. He even found time to serve as a juror.

He ran for the county register of deeds as a candidate for the Farmer's Alliance Party.[22] Local papers praised his abilities and integrity. The *Concordia Republican* wrote:

> *Mr. Woodruff is highly spoken of by all who know him as a good citizen and an honest man. He has been Trustee of Colfax Township for several years and has invariably given perfect satisfaction.*[23]

Even opposition papers in rival communities praised him. The *Clyde Republican* commented:

> *We have a man down in the Southwest corner of Colfax that has announced himself a candidate for Register of Deeds in the person of David Woodruff a man that has never applied for any state or county office, a man that is fully competent to fill the office and is well known throughout the county as being a man of good moral character and highly respected in his own neighborhood and a man that has filled the office of Trustee in his own township for at least five successive terms with credit to himself and satisfaction to his fellow townsmen. We don't wish*

---

22 An agrarian movement in the 1870s and 1880s that sought to improve economic conditions for farmers through the creation of cooperatives and political advocacy.

23 "News Items," *Concordia Republican*, Concordia, Kansas, 21 July 1881, page 5, column 3.

to say anything harsh of our neighbor Fry but don't like to see our friend B. waste his precious time to no purpose.[24]

Unfortunately, David's bid was unsuccessful; he finished fifth in the primary. There were allegations that the winning candidates had engaged in vote fixing. Though the Alliance Party offered to nominate him, David Woodruff declined, having agreed to abide by the results of the Republican primary.

Later, the *Kansas Kritic* wrote:

We know of no man in this part of the county whom we would sooner see in office than Mr. David Woodruff, nor one we would more heartily support.... But he was not defeated on account of incompetency or unworthiness but it was because he did not propose to conform to the rules and regulations of the political tricksters of these modern times.[25]

By now, the "Woodruff School" established by David had been operating successfully for well over a decade. Reports of the day stated that enrollment was unusually high and that David had even hired an assistant. (It is of interest that in 1883, the Washington School was built in Concordia—the first of four buildings in the city's present school system. The Woodruff School predates this by several years.)

The railroads brought rapid growth and prosperity to the region. Townships competed fiercely to be included as a railway stop. Miltonvale was chosen in 1882 as a station stop over Starr Township; as a result, Miltonvale thrived, and Starr became a ghost town. David Woodruff realized how important having a railway stop would be for his community, so in 1883, he organized a petition to the county commissioners to approve a bond so that the Salina, Lincoln and Fremont Railroad Company in Kansas could establish a rail line to

---

24 *Concordia Democrat*, Concordia, Kansas, 17 August 1881, page 4, column 2.
25 *Kansas Kritic*, Concordia, Kansas, 8 July 1885, page 4, column 2.

Colfax. The bond was approved, but the anticipated line never came. In 1887, the Atchison, Topeka, and Santa Fe Railway built a line farther north, running through Aurora, Huscher, and Concordia.

Two more children were welcomed into David's family: Emmette (4 August 1882) and Ethel Leona (9 October 1884). At one month old, Emmette became very ill and was not expected to live. However, he recovered and lived to adulthood. Emmette's older brother, Carl—David's oldest son—was not so fortunate. In January 1886, Carl fell ill and died, aged 12.

In 1885, David built a new home, which was described as one of the finest in the community. His wife, Victoria, helped with the planning, and David himself assisted the builders in the construction. This home cost over $1,000—a very large amount for one home at the time.

Two years later, while digging on his farm, David struck coal. This was tremendously good fortune. Wood was still in short supply, and the nearest dependable supply of coal was in Minersville, nearly 30 miles away.

In 1887, David decided to run for county office again, this time as county commissioner on the Republican ticket. The nomination process was beset with insider vote-swapping and deal-making. The delegation from Elk Township wanted their own man nominated for commissioner. Twenty votes were needed to secure the nomination; Elk and Starr townships together had 20 votes. After trying and failing to do away with the secret ballot, Elk Township made a deal with Starr Township: Elk would vote for Starr's candidate for county clerk, and Starr would vote for Elk's commissioner candidate.

Elk held up its end of the deal, but Starr Township reneged on its agreement. When the ballots were counted, it emerged that they had voted for David Woodruff, who was nominated on the first ballot.

Newspapers hailed the nomination. The *Clyde Herald* opined:

The truth is, it would have been hard to have selected a better man for that position anywhere; and we have every reason to believe he will deal out justice to all sections of his district.[26]

Woodruff was favored to win; many newspapers predicted an easy victory. But while he carried majorities in nearly every township, he lost heavily in Clyde, which voted decisively for his Democratic challenger, Borton. David Woodruff was defeated in his election bid by a mere 45 votes.

Despite this, David Woodruff had clearly established himself as a hardworking, prosperous farmer and a man of integrity. He was recognized as one of the leading figures in the county.

Anson Woodruff

Anson Woodruff settled away from his brothers, building a house in western Clyde. He maintained a very low public profile compared to his brother David. Occasional service as a juror, election official, or Republican political delegate was the extent of his public exposure. A drummer in the Civil War, he formed a city drum corps and performed in parades and celebrations, particularly on Decoration Day (now called Memorial Day). He eventually rented a farm outside the Clyde city limits late in 1887.

What his occupation was at this time is unclear. But in 1889 he was elected overseer of the AOUW (Advanced Order of United Workmen).[27]

Three more children were added to his family: Silas (12 February 1882), Annie May (16 July 1884), and Charles (4 January 1888). But mixed with this joy was tragedy: Annie May fell sick and died of brain fever, aged only eight months and two days.

---

[26] *Clyde Herald*, Clyde, Kansas, 14 September 1887, page 1, column 4.

[27] Founded in the United States and Canada after the American Civil War, this was the first of the "fraternal benefit societies"—organizations that offered insurance as well as sickness, accident, death, and burial policies.

Cloud County was transforming from a wild, empty prairie into a thriving community. Agriculture was well established, and the townships were experiencing the growing pains experienced by all new or maturing municipalities. Woodruffs added to the overall growth of both, and they themselves had been thriving.

But for the family, there were rough spots ahead.

Jamestown, circa 1899.

5
1890s: Growth and Hardship

The closing decade of the nineteenth century brought both innovations and turbulence. Basketball was invented. The General Electric Company was founded. Henry Ford built his first automobile. Hawaii was forcibly annexed by the United States. The Spanish-American War was fought, bringing new territories into America's possession (including Cuba and the Philippines). The American Anti-Imperialist League was established; members included such well-known figures as Mark Twain.

The Ringling Brothers Circus included Cloud County on their traveling circuit. In 1892, the circus train derailed east of Concordia. Heavy rains had loosened a small culvert, which collapsed when the engine passed over it, piling several cars in the stream. Two men were killed and four seriously injured; 20 horses perished. However, true to the motto "the show must go on," the circus performed in the city the following day to a crowd of four thousand spectators.

Aurora completed its local jailhouse in 1890. Situated on the southwest part of town, it was a small, squat structure built from hand-hewn limestone blocks and had a single barred window on each side.

Aurora Jail, on the southwest edge of the township.

Miltonvale was again ravaged by fire in 1890, destroying the grain elevator and livery stable.

The first successful telephone system in Cloud County, Concordia Telephone, was established in 1898; there were 93 subscribers. A group of women prohibitionists raided two Miltonvale saloons with hatchets, leaving an inch-deep pool of liquor spilled on the floor. The saloonkeeper in the second establishment accidentally shot a bystander and spent a year in jail. Clyde held its first annual Watermelon Festival, with nearly the entire county attending the event (over fifteen thousand were there).

Clyde experienced one of its coldest days on record in February 1899, when the temperature dropped to a frigid 33 degrees below zero Fahrenheit.

Locally, the 1890s began with promises of prosperity. The summer was cool, the winter mild. Harvests overall were excellent. Wheat yields averaged 23 bushels to an acre; in 1890, the state of Kansas harvested 275 million bushels of corn. Aside from some moderate hailstorms, the state overall was free from natural disasters.

The Woodruffs were now a formidable presence. Starting from the three brothers and one family who arrived in late 1871, there were 50 family members by the end of the decade. Woodruffs could be found not only in Colfax but also throughout much of the rest of the county, including Aurora, Clyde, Miltonvale, and Concordia.

The county continued to blossom and prosper; many Woodruffs contributed to that. But for the family as a whole, this was a rough stretch of years, filled with more than their fair share of hardships.

Hiram Woodruff

Most of Hiram's children were grown and raising families of their own. On 15 December 1890, his daughter Jessie married the Reverend Ulysses G. Travis—a big, red-headed man with a booming voice. Now only two of Hiram's children were left at the original homestead: Clark and Linnie.

Jessie's marriage to Ulysses on 15 November 1890 would prove to be the high point of Hiram's family fortunes for the coming decade. From that point on, a string of misfortunes ensued.

Jessie Woodruff and Ulysses Grant Travis. Ca. 1890.

Even at 70 years old, Hiram was still working his farm. Then, in July 1895 (aged 71), he caught his hand in some gears while adjusting some farm machinery. Several fingers were broken, and two fingers and part of his thumb were amputated. Within a month, another finger had to be amputated. Declining health over the following months reduced him to an invalid; at least four doctors attended him, and one declared him to be incurable. Finally, his health improved somewhat in 1901; while not fully recovered, he was at least not bedridden.

Unable to work the fields, Hiram received some financial relief from an unexpected source. In September 1896, he was finally granted his Civil War pension, which provided a small monthly income.

Hiram's extended family grew even larger. Isaac and wife, Mary Elizabeth, welcomed daughters Ruth (1894) and Cesil (1896) and sons Timothy (1897) and Joseph (1899). Then their oldest daughter, Ova, was stricken with diabetes. Insulin had not yet been discovered, and strict diets with minimal carbohydrate intake were the typical treatment.[28] The family doctor recommended feeding her rice. Isaac—whom relatives remembered as being ill-tempered and very tight with money—refused to pay the extra expense. Mary still managed to acquire and sneak rice into the house. It was not effective, however; Ova died in 1898, only 10 years old. She was buried in Nelson Cemetery on New Year's Day, 1899.

Hiram's son Albert welcomed several new children. In addition to eldest Ada Maude (born 1889), six more were born before the end of the century: George Albert (1890), Blanche (1892), Amanda Loverna (1893), Hazel (1895), Zaccheus (1898), and Rachel (1899).[29] Albert moved from Huscher to Concordia in December 1897, where Zaccheus and Rachel were born.

Son Lewis was also busy with a large family. He welcomed six children during this time: Albert (1890), Grace (1892), Hiram H. (1894), Cora May (1896), Harold H. (1898), and Esther (1899).

Jessie and Ulysses had two children before the turn of the century: Bessie (1893) and Ortha (1896).

---

28 This was not a cure; at best, it would buy the patients a few extra years of life.

29 The couple had briefly moved to California around 1888, then returned before 1892. Their first two children, Ada Maude and George Albert, were born in California.

Bessie Travis, 1911.

Rural living conditions at the end of the nineteenth century could be quite primitive. There was no electricity nor any of the conveniences it afforded. Cooking was done on wood or coal-fired stoves. Lack of indoor plumbing meant no running water in the home; this had to be fetched from outside at the well or stream. The toilet was the ubiquitous outhouse, which, if not properly placed, could pollute the drinking well. Disease outbreaks were common, including typhoid.

Hiram's family was one of those that became infected. In late 1899, his son Clark and daughter Dora were stricken with typhoid. Clark was deathly ill; he was not expected to live. Only a few weeks earlier, on 8 October 1899, Clark had married Marie ("Mamie") Mottin. Mamie, already pregnant, could not look after him for fear of endangering her life and that of their child. So Clark's younger sister, Linnie, cared for him, slowly nursing him back to health. Clark eventually recovered. But during this time, Linnie caught typhoid from her brother. After a short time, she died, at only 21 years of age.

Linnie Woodruff, 1895.

Clark Woodruff.

David Woodruff

The 1890s started off in a very promising way for David Woodruff and his family. He was well off financially. In the first year of the decade, he was extremely active in civic and political affairs, serving as juror, township officer, and member of the central committee of the Republican Party for Cloud County. He was even considered as a candidate for state senator.

Early in 1891, both he and his wife, Victoria, fell seriously ill; at the time, she was eight months pregnant. David was bedridden with heart disease. Four different doctors attended them; only one gave them any medicine. Victoria recovered first; their youngest daughter, Pearl, was born shortly after her recovery.

David, however, was an invalid for at least six months. After a couple months, he began slowly improving. By May, he was still confined to bed but was well enough to sit up in bed for part of each day. It was not until late in the summer that he had recovered sufficiently to get out of bed. By November, he was elected town clerk and was once again active in public affairs. The next year, he was appointed viewer[30] for a new planned road after the county commissioners approved the petition. At the same time, his eldest daughter, Lulu May, followed in her father's footsteps, enrolling in the Teacher's Institute.

In early January 1893, David's wife, Victoria, again fell suddenly ill. She died of blood poisoning (sepsis) only a few days later, leaving David to raise his two-year-old daughter, Pearl, alone. His eldest daughter, Lulu, became the "woman of the house," acting as surrogate mother and raising her younger siblings.

The combination of severe illness and the loss of one's wife was a double blow that might have crippled anyone's spirit. Yet within six months of his wife's death, David had recovered and was again active in the community.

---

30 Manager of the construction project.

David again dived headlong into local politics. Over the next several years he served as justice, treasurer, and assistant examiner for Colfax; he also served as juror for the township.

Several local organizations and groups benefited from his talents and energy. He taught at his own schoolhouse and was elected vice president[31] of the Cloud County Pioneers Association. He was also installed as an officer for the Miltonvale Lodge (No. 242) of the Masons.

Once again, David was a regular participant in local politics. However, his allegiance had changed. Up until 1890, he had been a staunch Republican. Now he was an active member of the Populist Party.[32] A frequent convention delegate, David served on many local and state party committees, ran as a People's Party candidate for local offices, and was even considered as a nominee for county supervisor.

Anson Woodruff

While Hiram and David were working their respective farms in the southeast portion of the county, younger brother Anson was living in the city of Clyde. He continued to keep a low public profile.

In 1892, Anson's Civil War pension was approved. This was good fortune, for he and Anna added three new children to the family: Bennie (1890), Lena (1892), and Fannie (1895). Sadly, Bennie died in September 1890, not quite six months old.

What kind of work he did after leaving Colfax is unknown. However, starting in 1897, he often went on extended hunting and trapping expeditions, frequently to Nebraska. From available accounts, this appeared to be his profession. He would often be gone for weeks at a time. During one such adventure, he was gone for an entire month and caught over 250 animals.

---

31 Each township elected a vice president. David Woodruff was vice president of Colfax.
32 A left-wing agrarian movement in the 1890s, promoting economic reform.

Nearly 30 years had passed since the Woodruff brothers' arrival in Cloud County. They had made an indelible mark on the area's development and history.

They had not finished helping shape the county. But they were aging, and their chapter was nearing its end. It was time for them to pass the baton to the next generation of Woodruffs.

Clyde, 1907.

6
1900s: The Next Generation

At the turn of the century, President McKinley was assassinated by an anarchist as the statesman reached out to shake his hand. Theodore Roosevelt assumed leadership of the nation. On the West Coast, the San Francisco earthquake nearly destroyed the city, killing over 3,000 and leaving three-quarters of the population homeless. The country's financial system nearly collapsed with the Panic of 1907; J. P. Morgan was instrumental in averting the disaster, shoring up the system with large sums of his own money and convincing others to do the same.

There was technological advancement and promise. The Ford Motor Company was established, introducing the Model T car. Wilbur and Orville Wright made their historic first powered flight at Kitty Hawk, North Carolina.

Cloud County's star was still rising. Concordia was thriving, boasting 4,600 residents, 1,200 homes, and miles of brick sidewalks. It had its own fire department, water company, and sewer system. There were now over 200 commercial establishments within the city limits.

Carrie Nation[33] visited Concordia and was warmly welcomed by many. Miltonvale installed its first telephone exchange in 1901.

The county's first pipe organ was installed at the Presbyterian church in Clyde on 1903. Miltonvale's grade school building, which had burned down, was replaced by a two-story brick building in 1905.

The Republican River, often subject to flooding, rose higher than ever before and broke through a dam near Concordia on 9 July 1902, re-routing its course by half a mile. The resulting flood caused a nearly complete failure of the watermelon crop.

The Woodruff line was now well into its second and third generations. The three original brothers had considerably slowed their public activities; sons and daughters were taking up the reins and contributing to the community.

Hiram Woodruff

After 30 years in Cloud County, Hiram and his family began migrating to California. In 1900, Cora Woodruff left Colfax and moved to Riverside. She was soon followed by father Hiram, brothers Isaac and Clark, and sister Dora.

As the twentieth century began, Hiram Woodruff was 75 years old. Since the farm accident that resulted in the amputation of his fingers, his health had been slowly declining. He remained an invalid for some time, although in 1901 he slowly started to improve. After Cora's departure, Hiram contemplated moving to California for

---

33 A radical prohibitionist, famed for attacking saloons with a hatchet.

health reasons. Finally, in September 1902, he moved to Riverside, California, where he resided until his death on 23 January 1904. One of Cloud County's earliest settlers and most productive farmers, he was buried in the old soldiers' section of Evergreen Memorial Park and Mausoleum in Riverside, California. His grave marker reads "Hiram Woodruff, Co. 1, Ohio Inf."

Hiram Woodruff and wife, Sarah Amanda (Gilmore) Woodruff. Circa 1900.

Isaac Woodruff

Isaac was next to relocate to the West Coast, although he returned after a short time. Selling his farm for $1,300, he moved to California in February 1903, working as a laborer building roads. His family (Mary Elizabeth and their five children) came with him. They traveled by train (Union Pacific), probably second or third class (always tight with money, Isaac almost certainly would not have paid for first-class tickets). The trip took roughly three days. One-way fares from Kansas to California were approximately $25 each, or $175 for the entire family.

Isaac and Mary Elizabeth had one more daughter in Kansas before they left: Dolly (Dorothea) Cornelia Woodruff, born in 1901. Isaac named her Baby Dolly, saying, "I can't be bothered to think of a name for another child." Dolly hated the name and always insisted on being called Dorothea.

His two youngest children, twins Alvin and Alma, were born on 31 July 1903, after the family's arrival in California. As the due date approached, Mary Elizabeth's sister Nellie came out from Kansas to be with her. Their mother had died giving birth to twins, so Nellie wanted Isaac to have a doctor in attendance. Isaac refused at first, arguing that his wife had already given birth to six children without any problems. But his sister-in-law held her ground. One day, she met Isaac at the front door and wouldn't let him in the house until he agreed; she even said she would call the police and threatened to hit him over the head with a chair. Finally, he agreed to pay for the doctor, although, according to family lore, "it nearly killed him."

Nellie's insistence saved the life of her sister. After the births, Mary Elizabeth began hemorrhaging. The doctor put blocks of wood under the foot of her bed, slowing the flow of blood. Mary Elizabeth recovered, but Isaac was enraged; he felt that all he had gotten for his $5.00 doctor's fee were two blocks of wood.

Public Sale

I am authorized to sell for Isaac Woodruff, at his farm three and one-half miles east of Huscher, and five miles north of Aurora, on

Thursday, Feb 12, 1903

commencing at one o'clock, the following property:

6 HEAD OF HORSES

1 span of mares 4 years old, weight 1101 lbs.
1 sorrel mare, weight about 1300 lbs.
1 black horse, weight about 1300 lbs.
1 black colt two years old.
1 black colt coming 1 year old.

4 HEAD MILCH COWS

1 full blood Jersey, 4 years old, fresh in February.
1 red cow, will be fresh in April.
1 red cow, now giving milk.
1 red cow, will be fresh in April.

14 HEAD OF HOGS

6 brood sows, 2 will farrow March 1st, the other 4 April 1st.
1 thoroughbred O. I. C. boar
7 shoats, weight about 180 lbs.

IMPLEMENTS, ETC.

4 dozen chickens
1 McCormick binder nearly new
1 McCormick mower, new

1 wagon as good as new
1 truck wagon and rack
1 Ohio riding cultivator
1 new walking cultivator
1 stalk cutter, 1 running gears
Sulky plow, walking plow, corn sheller,
Canton lister with drill combined,
Weed cutter, steel harrow,
New feed grinder,
Wheelbarrow, buggy, cart,
Set double harness, single buggy harness,
Single work harness, two stands bees.
2 or 3 tons cane hay, 6 or 7 tons prairie hay,
1 new Pioneer heater,
1 extension table, 1 drop leaf walnut table.
1 walnut bureau,
1 O. I. C. washer with new wringer.
Other household goods too numerous to mention.

USUAL TERMS WILL BE GIVEN

G. L. GREGG, Auct.

Auction, 5 Feb 1903. Isaac Woodruff's farm.

The two eldest girls, Cesil and Ruth, were put in charge of caring for the newborn twins as Mary recovered from the difficult birth. Ruth, who was always good with children, said, "I don't want a stinking old boy." So she cared for Alma, who turned out to be a fussy baby requiring lots of attention. Cesil took Alvin, who was quiet and peaceful. So when Cesil went outside to play, Ruth would pinch Alvin until he cried; then she would call her sister and say, "Your baby is crying."

The road work lasted close to a year, by which point Isaac could no longer support his family in Riverside. He is also recalled as saying that "California is no place to raise a family." He reasoned that on a farm, the family would at least have food and shelter. They returned to Kansas in early 1904, purchasing the Lange farm for $4,500. This may be the home that Mary Elizabeth called the "Spring Valley Farm." Their eldest daughter, Ruth, caught scabies removing wallpaper from one of the bedroom walls.

The house had a long front porch; the kitchen was in a separate building made of stone. There was an apple orchard in back, with a small stream (fed by a spring) running through the property. Mary Elizabeth would slice the apples and dry them on the stove; she did the same with some of the picked corn. These made excellent snacks for the children.

Mary Elizabeth began teaching in the district schools again, in addition to her work at home, including cooking and taking care of the farm and seven children. The move back from California to Kansas, plus the purchase of the farm, must have taken the last of their resources; Mary Elizabeth helped keep the family afloat during this time.

She was injured when the horse pulling her wagon was frightened by a car; the horse bolted and the wagon overturned. She suffered various injuries, including a broken limb.

Isaac Woodruff's Spring Valley Farm, circa 1925.

Modern view of Isaac's Spring Valley Farm, Aurora, looking North.

In general, the family was very poor. Isaac's daughters recall that, in their childhood, they never had toys to play with. Isaac was described as mean-spirited, tight with money, and an inept farmer;[34] he never played any great role in Cloud County affairs. His wife, Elizabeth, and his daughters made more of a contribution, teaching in the county schools of numerous townships. In contrast to her husband, Mary Elizabeth was described as kind-hearted, loving, generous, and very protective of the children.

Albert Earnest Woodruff

Albert had red hair and a beard. Family stories recall that he was nice to his children, played with them often, and was a loving father. His wife was Carrie Huscher, from the prominent Huscher family who had established the town of the same name.[35] Together, by the turn of the century, the couple had seven children. The youngest son, Zaccheus, died on 21 December 1900. He was buried on 23 December, the day before Christmas Eve, in Nelson, Kansas.

Over the next several years, they added five more to the family: Seth Rees (1901), Hildred (1904), Beulah F. (1906), Clarence (1908), and Benjamin Franklin (1909). Seth was reportedly handicapped. All told, there were 12 children from their marriage.

The family relocated to Topeka in 1903 but returned to Cloud County only four months later.

In addition to being deputy sheriff for Aurora Township, Albert—along with several of his children—played an important role in the establishment and operation of the county's rural telephone system.

---

[34] Newspapers sometimes would paint him as a prosperous farmer, usually when he went to the office to pay for a subscription.

[35] When the Atchison, Topeka, and Santa Fe Railway built a branch line through Huscher in 1887, it became a significant shipping point in the area.

Albert E. Woodruff and family, c. 1912.
Back row, L-R: Blanche Ada, Amanda Loverna, George, Ada Maude, Hazel.
Middle row, L-R: Hildred, Albert E., Rachel, Seth, Carrie Huscher, Beulah.
Front row, L-R: Clarence, Benjamin Franklin.

Concordia had established its own telephone system, the Concordia Telephone Company. Its rural competitor was the New Hope Telephone Company in the south. New Hope failed to get permission to expand into Concordia but put up poles and lines in the city anyway. Concordia's city council ruled that this was illegal and sent crews out to cut down the poles. A small war erupted between the two companies until the Kansas State Supreme Court ruled that New Hope could build in the city.

Albert ran the New Hope office; later, he was a lineman for the company and eventually took charge of its central office. Hazel later headed the New Hope headquarters. Ada Maude worked for Daugherty Telephone as a "central girl" (switchboard operator).

Lewis Woodruff

Typhoid had not yet finished with Hiram's family. Lewis Woodruff's son Harold was stricken in 1901, as was Lewis himself a few years later. Lewis was ill for weeks; after nearly a month, he was able to get out again.

Like many of the Woodruffs, he played baseball. In 1901, he signed up as a catcher for the Boston Bloomers baseball team.[36] He toured with them for at least one season.

Alice had two more children, twins born on 21 December 1905: Naomi and Joshua. Unfortunately, Joshua died the same day.

By this time, Lewis's older children were nearly grown. Albert and Grace passed their common school[37] examinations in 1908. Albert also earned his teacher's certificate only a few months later. Nevertheless, he did not immediately secure a teaching position and continued working on the farm.

Clark Woodruff

In 1900—the year after Clark recovered from his near-fatal attack of typhoid—his only child, Julius, was born. Clark kept a low profile over the next decade. However, he was an avid photographer, often taking photos in town of buildings, bands, celebrations, and people. The local papers occasionally published some of the more newsworthy shots.

---

36 A women's barnstorming baseball club, often with men on the roster. They would play local city teams, college and even semi-pro opponents.

37 A free public school available to all students aged five to 18 years. Taught through eighth grade.

In 1909, he moved his family to a new home in Miltonvale. While mixing plaster for the outside walls, he was knocked down by a bolt of lightning. He and the others helping him were not seriously injured, but they were deeply shaken for some time afterwards.

Clark Woodruff with wife Marie (Mamie) Mottin, son Julius. Ca. 1904.

Della, Dora, and Florence Woodruff

In 1905, Della Woodruff died of dropsy (edema), one year after her father Hiram. She was only 47 years old and had lived in Huscher for more than 20 years. Married to Joseph B. Campbell, one of the area's wealthier farmers, she was known all over the county for her kindness and charming disposition. Her funeral was the largest ever seen in Nelson Township.

Florence Woodruff appears to have traveled to California as early as the mid-1890s, though whether she relocated or merely visited there is unclear. She married James C. Fox in California in 1896. She died in 1909.

Dora Woodruff also moved to California, probably around the time of her father's death. In 1903, Isaac and Sarah Amanda Woodruff deeded the original homestead to their youngest son, Clark, for $1,600. Sarah Amanda continued to live there while Hiram was in California. In February 1906, she came back to Kansas to visit her mother, Sarah (Gilmore) Woodruff. The two returned together to California. Four months later, she (Dora) married James Franklin Hawkins in Riverside in 1906. Two children were born in quick succession: Alma May (1907) and Clarence E. (1909).

David Woodruff

While David Woodruff had slowed his civic activities due to age and poor health, he did not abandon them entirely. He started the new century as a juror in the county court (once in 1900 and again in 1904). He did attend one county political convention and was appointed to one of the committees. But this was the extent of his involvement for several years; he devoted more time to his personal affairs. During this time, he took a trip back to Barlow Township, Ohio, to visit his father, Silas Woodruff. Silas, aged 91, was very ill and not expected to recover. Fortunately, Silas did regain his health before the end of David's stay.

Surprisingly, starting in 1905, David had a burst of activity, both personal and public, that lasted for three years. This involved some major (and unexpected) changes. He successfully petitioned the county commissioners to build a bridge in the southeast part of the county. He was also a candidate for justice of Elk Township. But this time he was running on the Democratic ticket—a shocking change for a lifelong Republican.

He also bought a house and seven acres in Clyde Township in November of the same year. His intentions were to spend the winter in Clyde, then to sell the farm that he and his brother Hiram had built and which he had successfully worked since his arrival in Cloud County.

Limestone arch bridge, Ames township. Built ca. 1900.

AUCTION:

I will sell at auction at my farm,
FOUR MILES NORTH & ½ MILE WEST
OF MILTONVALE

TUESDAY, NOVEMBER, 14th.

THE FOLLOWING PROPERTY

8 Yearling Steers; 7 Spring Steer Calves; 5 Spring Heifer Calves; 2 Cows; and 3 Yearling Heifers. 1 Sorrel Work Horse, 12 Years old; 1 Bay Brood Mare, 14 Years old; 1 Bay Horse Colt, 3 Years old; 1 Black Work Horse, 6 Years old; 1 Buck-skin Mare Colt, 1 yr. old; 1 Bay Mare Colt, 1 yr. old; 1 Black Horse Colt, 1 yr. old and Some Duroc Jersey Hogs.

Some Harness; 1 150 egg Sure Hatch Incubator; 1 Heating Stove; and other articles too numerous to mention.

SALE BEGINS AT ONE O'CLOCK SHARP.

TERMS On sums of $10.00, and under, Cash.
On sums over $10.00, a credit of 12 months will be given on approved notes bearing 10 per. cent interest from date.
Two per cent off sums over $10.00, for cash.

DAVID WOODRUFF,
owner.

Notice of auction, David Woodruff's farm, 10 Nov 1905.

Arthur C. Woodruff

Arthur, like his father, was active in the local elections, acting as a clerk. In the spring of 1903, he and his family moved to Topeka, Kansas. Several months later, they moved back to Huscher.

In 1904, they began working a farm on a river bottom near Clyde. They were flooded out in November 1905. He and his family moved to his father's farm, delaying David's sale of the property by two years.

Later, Arthur consulted a local doctor in Concordia, apparently for hearing problems.

Lulu Woodruff

In 1900, Lulu May ("June") Woodruff married Ambrose Booten Fry Jr., son of A. B. Fry Sr. The Frys were another prominent Cloud County family; they arrived in 1873, shortly after the Woodruffs. His father, A. B. Fry Sr., was active in politics. In 1904, he was the Democratic candidate for probate judge.

That same year, A. B. Fry Jr. was cleaning a shotgun at home. Apparently still loaded, it accidentally discharged; the buckshot went through a thin partition, striking Lulu in the breast and head. Thirty-six pieces of buckshot were extracted. The wounds, although not considered serious, were quite painful. Lulu lost an eye in the incident and wore a glass eye for the rest of her life.

Edmond Silas Woodruff

In 1895, at the age of 17, Edmond Silas procured the position of postman, working the route between St. Joseph and Clyde (a 10-mile distance). While the locations would change over the years, Edmond would remain a familiar and dependable face for the post office, delivering mail in the area for decades to come.

His uncle, Anson Woodruff, had been one of the first three carriers appointed to the newly established RFD (Rural Free Delivery) routes from the Clyde post office. In July 1902, Anson retired from his route due to health conditions, and Edmond replaced him on this route.

Deliveries were originally made in a horse-drawn wagon. There were no paved or gravel roads, only country lanes of dirt or mud, depending on the weather. Edmond's route crossed the Republican River; many times, he was unable to complete his route due to high water and flooding. At one point, in summer 1905, the flooding was so extensive that the mail could not be delivered across the river for eight days, bridge or no bridge. There were times, however, when he was determined to complete his rounds and succeeded despite these barriers of nature. One time he left his wagon on one side of the river, crossed the bridge over the flooded river by foot, and delivered the mail on foot. At times he resorted to using a bicycle.

It was difficult work. Edmond described his experiences:

I then became a rural mail carrier out of Clyde. I had many experiences in my 31 years, four and one-half months, striving to get the mail to my patrons. I endured the cold and blizzards of the winters, having to shovel my way through the snow-drifts a great many times. One day, I was "blizzard-bound" when partway around the route and stayed the night with one of my good patrons. I crossed the flooded Republican River many times and have "plowed" through deep mud all around my route, as there were no graveled, or paved roads, in that part of the country at this early date.[38]

At the end of 1905, the post office determined that Edmond's designated route was not feasible, for two reasons. First, the mail delivery schedule via trains to and from Concordia did not allow for

---

[38] A. L. Sheppard, *Woodruff Family History*, unpublished manuscript (n.d.). Notes by Edmond Silas Woodruff.

frequent delivery. Second, the frequent flooding of the Republican River too often prevented delivery to patrons. So the route was moved from Clyde to Ames, five miles away but on the same side of the river as the families it served. Edmond remained the carrier, though he now had to leave home at 3:00 every morning to travel to Ames to start his rounds.

Delivering mail by horse-drawn wagon to rural farms spaced a half-mile or more apart, he handled over 12,000 pieces of mail each month, rain or shine. His patrons appreciated his tireless work and often gave him gifts in gratitude. One Christmas, for example, he received a variety of gifts from various homes, including a dressed chicken, part of a side of beef, a collection of mincemeat, and "one of the best dinners he [Edmond] had ever had the pleasure of eating." Another patron decided to give him a flock of chickens and, not wanting to weigh him down with the present, hauled it several miles to town and delivered it to Edmond's residence.

Edmond was well paid. For delivering the mail, he received $900 per year—twice the average national income at the time. Postal employees in Clyde were paid based on the income of the post office. In 1910, his salary was raised to $1,000 per year.

Well established in his professional career, he started a family. He married his childhood sweetheart, Cora Buell, in 1903. Shortly afterwards, they had their first two children: Beulah Luretta (1905) and Lillian Victoria (1907).

He participated in many social and church affairs. He was elected senior deacon of the local Masonic lodge. An accomplished singer, he would regularly perform at church services, school functions, and various public events. When his niece, Lena Woodruff, graduated from Clyde High School, he was the featured vocalist for the ceremony. He performed not only at Presbyterian but also at Baptist services. He often appeared onstage at Concordia's Wonderland Theater.

Emmette Woodruff

In 1902, at the age of 21, Emmette Woodruff married Ruby Woodworth, member of another prominent family in Cloud County, with roots dating back to Plymouth Colony in 1607. Her father, Curtis W. Woodworth, regularly contributed to public affairs, acting as school officer and assessor and running for public office, eventually replacing David Woodruff as Colfax trustee after Woodruff's death.

Emmette and Ruby immediately started building their family. Three daughters were born in quick succession: Leah Anna (1903), Gladys (1904), and Doris Nola (1905). The couple's last child, Allie Imogene, was not born until 1908.

In 1907, Emmette auctioned off livestock and farm equipment and purchased a joint interest in the Heald Brothers Meat Market. He ran this interest together with a partner, selling meats of all kinds to the public and providing meat to the poor. He built a nice home in town.

LACY & WOODRUFF

The new proprietors at the City Meat Market keep constantly on hand a full line of Fresh and Salt Meats of all kinds. Fish and Oysters in their season. When you have hogs or cattle to butcher let us do the work. Highest Cash Prices Paid For Hides.

At Heald Bros old stand.

1907 advertisement for Emmette Woodruff's meat market.

Heald Meat market, prior to 1908. The two men are probably the Heald Brothers.

The year 1908 saw a reversal of fortune for Emmette. After 18 months of ownership, he suddenly sold his interest in the meat market for unknown reasons. In the same month (May 1908), his daughters fell ill. He resorted to doing carpenter work, often out of town; his wife and daughters would often visit Ruby's parents and stay with them during this time.

It appears that Emmette was struggling financially. Their youngest daughter, Allie Imogene, was born 28 October 1908. Three weeks later, Emmette sold their property. At the same time, Ruby Woodruff was admitted to the Clay Center hospital; she stayed there for two months

In April 1909, Emmette left town "to solicit for a picture making concern"—a business dealing with photo enlargements. That was the last time anyone is known to have seen or heard from him. Ruby was left to raise their daughters alone. Two months after Emmette disappeared, daughter Allie Imogene contracted cholera infantum[39] and died after only 10 hours.

Emmette's brother, Edmond Silas Woodruff, became guardian of Emmette and Ruby's children. Ruby often visited her sister in Vancouver, usually taking daughter Leah with her.

Ethel Woodruff

In March 1903, Ethel Woodruff married Ray Austin, a veteran of the Philippine-American War. The wedding took place at the home of her father, David Woodruff. After the ceremony, they temporarily stayed with Ray Austin's parents near Miltonvale. Shortly after the wedding, Ethel fell ill. By the end of June, she was slowly improving and eventually was able to get out again.

They had their first two children—Erma Vera Austin (1904) and Lawrence Woodruff Austin (1906).

Anson Woodruff

As soon as the first winter of the new century melted away, Anson embarked on a two-month trapping expedition in Nebraska.

In March of the next year (1901), the Clyde post office established the new RFD (Rural Free Delivery) routes. Routes were structured to most effectively carry out the daily routine. New wagons were purchased and specially painted as official mail vehicles. Anson Woodruff was one of the original three carriers for this new service. He began making a list of families who wanted mail delivered. Families put up delivery boxes on the public roads by their farms;

---

39 An often fatal form of gastroenteritis occurring in infants. It did not have the same cause as cholera but had somewhat similar characteristics. Common in the nineteenth century but now rare.

newspaper articles were published instructing people not to meddle with or destroy the public mailboxes.

The new RFD routes were officially to begin on 1 June 1901. They actually started on 17 May 1901, two weeks ahead of schedule. In the first month, Anson delivered and collected 1,954 pieces of mail along his route. He sold his house west of Clyde and bought a new residence in town on Campbell Avenue for $1,000. Although he lived within the city limits, this was still a farming community; many families kept farm animals on their property. Anson kept a pet donkey for his children. One day it wandered off and was run over by a train.

The latter part of 1901 saw Anson's health start to decline. He began suffering from neuralgia. The next year, he was again on the sick list; his nephew Edmond delivered the mail for him. Anson officially resigned as mail carrier in July 1902, after only one year of service; Edmond officially replaced him.

After retirement, and despite his health problems, Anson remained an active outdoorsman. He continued trapping and fishing in surrounding areas. On one expedition, he caught 30 pounds of fish without a pole, using his bare hands. These expeditions served as a source of income to supplement his Civil War pension; he sold the pelts and the fish. It is reported that he once sold $14 worth of fish in three days—more than two weeks' income for a farm worker of the time.

He was also active in Clyde's annual Watermelon Festival, which started around 1899 and is still held today after 120 years. Soil in the county's low-lying areas was excellent for growing the fruit, and watermelon fields abounded. Anson participated for many years, hauling wagonloads of melons to the festivities. His son Charles would later contribute to the festival as well, bringing the delicious fruit to the celebration.

Anson's health waxed and waned. He fell ill several times. Once, after an illness, he fell asleep while driving his wagon and smoking a cigar. The blanket he was wearing caught fire, burning his hands. It could have been even more serious, but, fortunately, his horse ran into a snowbank, extinguishing the fire.

He and his family moved several times during these years. He had sold his home and purchased another one in the city. In 1904, his house was struck by lightning. He alternated between city and country, living on farms from time to time. In 1910, he rented the farm belonging to his brother David.

Anson's children, James, Silas, and Lena Woodruff, excelled in school, in the Woodruff tradition. Lena's attendance in particular was so consistently punctual that when she was late one day, it warranted an article in the newspaper.

Silas was a prominent figure in high school, becoming president of both the Senior Forensic Division and the Literary Society. He was also selected to give an oration for the midyear program and could be seen on the football field playing for the school.

While Silas excelled in academics, his brother Charles eclipsed him on the gridiron, starring at left half. Playing for Clyde High School, his team went undefeated and were considered one of the best high school teams in the state. This was in the early days of the sport, when it was rough and dangerous. More than once, Charles was reported to have come off the field with a black eye.

The Railroads

Railroads were crucial arteries for the county—a fast, efficient, and reliable method of transporting people and goods to the rest of the country.

Anson's children worked for the railroads, at various places along the lines. James was a relief agent for Santa Fe. Silas Woodruff worked as the night agent at the Missouri Pacific Railroad depot, not only in Clyde but also at stations in Gardner, Osborne, and Stockton.

Missouri Pacific Railroad Depot in Concordia, Kansas.

The life of a rural railroad agent on the night shift was generally quiet. However, for Silas, there was one notable exception. At 2:00 a.m. on Friday, 8 August 1902, Silas was on his shift at the train depot, taking a nap. He awoke to find two masked men standing over him and pointing a handgun at him. The men ordered him to open the safe. When he insisted that he did not know the combination, they swore at him for some time, then ordered him to lay still and put a pillow over his head, which he did. They then gathered up whatever money they could find, emptying the change drawer. They removed his trousers and took $1.85 that Silas had in one pocket. At that point, they wished him a good morning and left.

Silas immediately went to report the robbery. However, he discovered that the robbers had also taken his pants, so he made a "record breaking sprint" to the sheriff's office. The next day, the two men were arrested and held for trial at $1,000 bail each.

Had the robbers been able to access the safe, they would have found $20,000 inside. They also overlooked the $5.25 stashed in Silas's other pocket.

County Telephone Service

Woodruffs were still keeping the local telephone service working. Several family members worked in the central office. At one point, there were four Woodruffs on the switchboards: Ada, Hazel, Blanche, and Amanda. Between them, they operated the central office 24 hours a day. Harold was a bookkeeper. George Woodruff worked as a lineman; Albert Woodruff fixed phones, worked the switchboard, and was also a lineman. In 1911, however, Albert had a serious accident. Working on external telephone lines, he slipped and fell across a pair of live 2,200-volt power lines. Fortunately, he was able to get a passerby to call the electric company to have the power shut off. Miraculously, he survived, but he was seriously injured. When he was pulled from the lines, he was unconscious and his clothes were smoking. He was badly burned on the back and thigh; one finger was charred all the way to the bone. He sued the Concordia Electric Light Company for $5,000 in damages. The suit was later settled out of court, and the company paid Albert's doctor bills and attorney fees, amounting to $70. He resigned his position with the telephone company one year later, due to health issues caused by the accident.

Other family members from Ohio had also come west and settled in Cloud County. One was Sarah Springer, widow of Matthew Woodruff;[40] she arrived in the 1880s with her two sons, Jesse and Mark.

Jesse Woodruff did not figure in Cloud County's history to any great extent. For the most part, he was a traveler, frequently working for the railroads. He did work for the Santa Fe, B & M, and Missouri Pacific. In between, he held a variety of jobs, including clothing-store salesman, store clerk, and laborer at a lumber yard.

He was frequently out of town. In the span of 18 months (1889–1890), he traveled to various parts of Kansas, Nebraska, Wyoming, Missouri, Colorado, Minnesota, and other locations both east and west. Often, he stayed and worked there for short periods of time. There are reports that he made extended trips in both directions. Once he traveled to Louisville, Kentucky, to work at a retail establishment, only to find when he arrived that it had burned to the ground the day before.

He still managed to make frequent trips home to visit family, particularly his mother. At these times, he also often played on the city baseball teams with his brother Mark.

---

40 Matthew was a cousin of Anson, David, and Hiram.

Finally, in July 1890, he relocated to Pueblo, Colorado. While he was en route, the hotel where he was staying in Como, Colorado, caught fire, but he managed to escape without injury. In Pueblo, he married Ella Marlatt, a former schoolteacher from Concordia. They eventually moved to Ogden, Utah, where he was engaged in the mining industry.

Brother Mark, by contrast, was deeply immersed in public affairs. Originally a printing apprentice in Keokuk in 1880, he worked as a journeyman printer. After his family moved to Concordia, he made his mark on several of the local papers. He managed the *Portis Patriot*, eventually purchasing it; he occasionally edited the *Concordia Daily Blade* when they needed help. He moved from Concordia to Jamestown, where in 1888, he started a new publication, *The Quill*, eventually becoming both proprietor and editor. (In 1889, he sold his interest in *The Quill*.) He was known for his sharp and biting editorial style. He then became editor of the *Concordia Daylight*. He later did work for the *Burr Oak Herald*.

He was a thin man, described as a "featherweight." And he sported a mustache that must have been quite prominent. Once, after shaving it off, he was denied admittance to a private dance because the doorman did not recognize him.

Despite his thin physique, he was still athletic, regularly playing for both Jamestown and Concordia city baseball teams and briefly acting as captain for the latter. He served as umpire for some games. He was once accused of throwing a game for $85; this was never proved, and one paper labeled it as probably false.

Apparently, he had a brash nature. Described as a "masher," he was prone to poor behavior. He was a frequent drinker; he would travel from Jamestown to Concordia to drink there. There are several accounts of him being extremely intoxicated and, at least once, vomiting on the street. Sometimes friends would carry him home unconscious after a bender and put him to bed. One time he attempted to kill a stray cat in the street with his revolver. The shot penetrated the wall of a nearby building, lodging in the pillow beneath the head of a sleeping child.

Despite his colorful and controversial nature, he was still liked and respected by many. He was prominent both socially and civically. He performed in several local stage productions. Politically, he was extremely active. He devoted much of his energy to the Republican Party, from the Young Men's Republican Club to county delegate to the state convention. He launched several unsuccessful bids to become a councilman for Concordia. In 1889, he became city clerk in Jamestown. He was also commissioned as a third corporal in the Kansas National Guard.

He associated with James E. Hageman (son of James M. Hageman, a key figure in the county's early history). He was also a member of the coroner's jury for the inquest into the death of "Coffeepot" Johnson.[41]

In 1890, Concordia was the victim of embezzlement twice within a span of only a few weeks. The second case involved the city clerk suddenly leaving with $2,000 of city funds in his pocket. An editorial in the *Concordia Daylight* by Mark Woodruff implied that Concordia mayor Dan Brown colluded with the criminals.[42]

Mayor Brown entered the newspaper office and knocked Mark to the floor. A fistfight ensued. The mayor was large and heavy, but despite Mark's featherweight build, he held his own—until the mayor pulled a gun. Pointing it at Mark, the mayor demanded that he write a retraction of the article or he would kill him. Mark meekly complied, although later he stated in print that he "retracted my retraction."[43]

---

41 Accounts vary on exactly how "Coffeepot" Johnson acquired his name. He was a Swedish immigrant. One day he was camping by Buffalo Creek; two Indians entered his camp, drank the coffee he was brewing on the fire, and smashed the utensils. Johnson reportedly stood and yelled at them in his native tongue; they were so surprised that they returned the coffeepot and departed, leaving him unharmed.

42 Mayor Brown appointed the city clerk and, although the city council refused to confirm him, kept him in office without any bond.

43 Mark kept his word, technically speaking. The mayor demanded that he write a retraction, which he did. But there is no evidence that he ever published it.

As soon as the mayor left the office, Mark immediately swore out a complaint. Brown was arrested for assault and attempt to kill and bound over for trial. He was eventually acquitted, based on the fact that the jurors did not know whether the gun was loaded. Following the trial, he was immediately rearrested on the charge of assault and battery, to which he pleaded guilty and paid a fine of $25. Several of the local papers published editorials disagreeing with the verdict, stating unequivocally that it was a miscarriage of justice and that Dan Brown was guilty.

Four months later, Mark left with his mother for Colorado Springs, Colorado. He worked for two newspapers there: the *Evening Telegraph* and the *Pueblo Chieftain*. He briefly became a miner and worked at the famous Last Chance Mine. Entering politics again, he was elected county clerk of Mineral County. He was then personally appointed postmaster of Creede, first by President McKinley and then by President Roosevelt. He became secretary of the State Land Office for four years, when he resigned in 1906 to accept the position of superintendent of Pike's Peak and Plum Creek Forest Reserve.

Eight months later, he suddenly resigned his position, via telegraph. He gave no reason for stepping down. At this point, Mark Woodruff effectively disappeared.

Shortly afterwards, discrepancies were discovered in the Land Office Records. An investigation uncovered altered records and land fraud involving 100,000 acres of state land. Federal authorities began looking for Mark Woodruff. Charges of embezzlement and fraud were filed. There were indications that not only he but others higher up in the state administration were involved. Reports were published of his whereabouts, from Nevada to Alaska to Honolulu.

Finally in 1909, Mark was arrested in Plattesville, Colorado. For the previous two years, he had been living in Portland, Oregon, and working on the local papers. Charges of embezzlement were dismissed, as the statute of limitations had expired. But he was still charged with forgery for altering state records. Eventually, these charges were also dismissed, possibly in the hope that he would turn state's evidence and implicate others. He had reportedly threatened to implicate Colorado's former governor and secretaries of state.

However, when he appeared in court to testify, he refused to answer any questions on advice of counsel, to prevent self-incrimination. He gave the investigation nothing to go on, and in October 1909, Mark Woodruff left the courthouse a free man. One of the local Concordia papers reported:

> *The company he kept was not of the best but he was never considered a man that would get into this trouble.*[44]

Even as the Woodruffs built up their communities, individual family members continued gradually to migrate away from Cloud County. Arthur Woodruff moved to a farm in Cherryville, Montgomery County. Harold ventured farther away, purchasing land in Arizona for his home. James moved to Little Rock, Arkansas, where he was station agent for the railroad and also ran a shoe store. Esther moved to Idaho with her parents, as did Hazel. Silas immigrated to Muskegon, Michigan, and worked in vaudeville. He later settled in Chicago, worked as a policeman, and studied dentistry.

Despite the attrition, the Woodruffs were still a large presence and had many more contributions to make in the area in the coming decade.

---

44 "Was a Defaulter," *Concordia Empire*, Concordia, Kansas, 1 July 1909, page 5, column 3.

Clyde, 1910.

7
1910s: Zenith

The decade of the "Teens" brought progress and historic events, as well as death and tragedy on a scale not seen since the Middle Ages. The Boy Scouts of America was founded. The first Indianapolis race was held. Ford introduced the assembly line, mass producing cars that ordinary people could afford. A new Model T Ford could be obtained direct from the factory for $780—half the cost of the new Hudson 33, which sold for $1,500. Henry Ford also raised minimum pay for his factory workers to $5 a day. The Panama Canal was finished and began operations.

The Federal Reserve was established. After the Panic of 1907, there was a debate over whether to change the size of US banknotes (this was not done until 1929). Theodore Roosevelt ran unsuccessfully as a third-party candidate for president, paving the way for Woodrow Wilson's victory.

The *Titanic* struck an iceberg, sinking with over 1,500 lives lost. Pancho Villa began raiding towns in the United States, attacking Columbus, New Mexico.

Cloud County had reached its zenith; the 1920 census recorded 18,388 residents. This was as large as the county's population would ever get; thereafter, it began a slow and steady decline that continues to this day. There were two main causes for the population loss. The first was that residents migrated from rural to urban areas looking for work, usually in something other than farming (which was always extremely demanding). This has always been a factor in people leaving rural areas. The second cause was that the establishment of railroads facilitated access to nearly every location in the country.

The value of all farm products produced there that year, including livestock, was nearly $5,000,000. Corn, wheat, oats, hay, and Irish potatoes were the main crops.

Weather in Cloud County has always been a factor to be reckoned with, and this decade was no exception. In May 1905, rain fell for a month without stopping. The Republican River, frequently known to overflow, flooded Concordia and nearby towns, causing a catastrophe not seen before or since. Water flow was measured at over 160 times its normal volume. The river crested at 23 feet and spanned up to four miles wide. The sheer volume of water was enough to effectively change the stream channel through town. Hundreds of people were killed, tens of thousands of cattle were lost, and over 270 acres of farmland were destroyed. Then, in 1912, the county saw a major blizzard. In Concordia, snowbanks were as high as people's heads.

The most catastrophic (and well-known) event to occur was the coming of World War I, the "war to end all wars." This was the bloodiest war the United States had experienced up to that point; around the world, 17 million were killed. Dovetailed in this was the "Spanish Flu." In all, 675,000 Americans died of this new and frightening disease; up to 50 million people died worldwide. Coincidentally, this disease is closely tied to the history of Cloud County.

1910s: ZENITH

The three original brothers were no longer movers and shakers in local affairs. Hiram moved to California in 1902 and died two years later.

David Woodruff

Left: David Woodruff with a cousin, circa 1914.

David's health had been declining for a few years. In 1911, he suffered an apoplectic stroke and was no longer mentally capable of looking after his own business interests. During one of his lucid intervals, he asked Judge Fry to have a guardian appointed to care for his interests. David's family agreed that this was the best decision. An insanity trial was held as a formality; David's friend James Neill was appointed guardian, and David moved to a sanitarium for rest and treatment.

He suffered two more strokes, the last of which was in late 1914. He was moved to his son Edmond's home, where he remained until his death on 8 October 1914. He was buried in Miltonvale Cemetery beside his wife, Victoria. Thus, Cloud County lost the second (and most influential) of the three Woodruff brothers.

David left a large estate (homes in Clyde and Colfax and nearly 600 acres of land); his son Edmond was appointed estate administrator. But due to complications, the estate could not be settled for nearly five years.

Now the children and grandchildren fully held the reins, free to make their own marks on the communities. While their fathers had helped build the county largely by establishing agriculture and the civil service, the new generations pursued other avenues. Some did perform civic duties (such as mail delivery or road maintenance), but in the main, they engaged in commercial enterprise, religion, and enriching lives through the arts.

Edmond Silas Woodruff

Edmond Silas Woodruff had been a stable fixture in the Clyde post office for some time. By now, he had become quite innovative in devising efficient methods to deliver mail to his rural patrons. He set aside the horse-drawn wagon in favor of an Indian motorcycle. He also delivered the mail via boat, bicycle, car, and even horseback, depending on the year and road conditions. His patrons, thankful for his efforts, frequently rewarded him with gifts of food and drink—very much appreciated during the cold winter months.

Edmond was described as "a little man, 32 inches around and skinny as a jack rabbit." Devoutly religious, he grew tired of the other mail carriers swearing. He once bet them 50 cents that they could not refrain from swearing for one week. He was happy to lose the bet.

He would start his rounds on the far end of his route and then work his way home. He would take the early morning train to the post office; once he hauled a car from Clyde to Ames on a railroad push car to use for mail delivery. The local Catholic priest, Father Emery, purchased a boat for mail delivery, presumably for use when the river was at high water and bridges were impassable. Edmond even built a house on top of his Ford sedan to protect him from bad weather during his deliveries.

In July 1919, the rural mail carriers formed a union. Ed Woodruff, as a veteran mail carrier, was active in its formation.

Ed was very fond of motorcycles. He would ride them for pleasure and drove one on his mail route. In 1914, he took his Harley-Davidson on a month-long, 900-mile trip along rough dirt roads to visit family in Ohio. He returned by train, shipping his motorcycle back to Kansas. He said it was too hard to push through the dust in Missouri, Illinois, and Ohio.[45]

Being a rural mail carrier put tremendous demands on his time, yet he apparently inherited his father's almost inexhaustible energy and drive. Edmond dove into business, establishing local franchises selling Goodyear tires and Harley-Davidson motorcycles and parts. He even found time to delve into politics and the arts.

---

45 *Voice-Republican*, Clyde, Kansas, 27 August 1914, page 1, column 6.

Advertisement, Edmond S. Woodruff, authorized Goodyear tire dealer. 25 March 1915.

Performing Arts

Edmond was a talented and accomplished singer. He was described as having a soft, rich tenor voice and interpreting music very well. His talents were in great demand: he sang regularly for both Presbyterian and Methodist church services. He performed at many public functions, such as grand openings, holiday celebrations, and school graduations. He was even billed at the Wonderland Theater in Concordia—one of the region's most prestigious venues at the time for performances and film screenings.

Edmond S. Woodruff performing at Wonderland Theater, 22 June 1911.

His daughter, Beulah, grew up with a fine voice and often sang with her father. She was a skilled musician, sometimes publicly performing on piano.

Anson cultivated a love of music in his family. He bought a piano for his daughters. Music classes were often held at his home. One of his daughters, Lena, would become an acclaimed musician in her own right. She performed several times at the Wonderland Theater in Concordia, starting when she was a teenager.

After graduating high school, she attended the normal college and embarked on a teaching career. She did not abandon her music. She studied music at Bethany College in Lindsborg, Kansas. She was proficient on several instruments, including violin. However, she excelled on keyboards, playing piano and organ. At the college, out of all the keyboardists, she was chosen to perform Handel's *Messiah*. At graduation, she delivered an oration on "Why We Should Study Music."

Her talents were in great demand; she regularly played for school functions, church services, public events, weddings, and other private services.

In tandem with her regular teaching duties, she gave private music lessons, played organ for the Presbyterian church, and continued giving recitals and public performances.

In 1916, a benefit musical was given for Lena in appreciation of her talent and musical contributions to the community. The local paper reported: "In Miss Lena Woodruff, Clyde has a musician she should be justly proud of."[46] In their critique, *The Farmers' Voice* commented:

> *Miss Woodruff proved herself an artist of rare ability… Her pipe organ numbers were particularly inspiring and revealed the interpretation of a real artist.*[47]

---

46 *Clyde Voice-Republican*, Clyde, Kansas, 20 June 1916, page 1, column 4.
47 *The Farmers' Voice*, 4 July 1916, page 1 column 2.

Lena Woodruff, High School graduation photo, 22 May 1911.

Education

No discussion of Cloud County education is complete without mention of the Woodruffs. Starting in the 1870s, the family built and ran schools, teaching students in the region.

Now, with Cloud County at its zenith, they were, without doubt, a driving educational force. As many as eight Woodruffs taught school simultaneously in various cities and townships.[48] Sometimes the classes included their own family members—cousins and even brothers or sisters.

The family excelled at this profession. Cesil Woodruff was appointed as one of the officers overseeing the spelling contests. She attended the first session of the Teacher's Institute held in the county. Albert, Grace, Lena, and Fannie attended subsequent sessions. Fannie was elected vice president of the Cloud County Teacher's Association. Several (Cesil, Grace, Cora, and Fannie) administered graduation examinations.

In 1915, the average pay for a teacher was around $70 per month—not generous but much better than the average farm laborer's wage at the time.

Isaac Woodruff's main contribution to Cloud County was his two daughters, Ruth and Cesil, who educated so many children in numerous townships.

Ruth first taught in 1912 at School District No. 7 with 22 students. (The following year, Cesil would teach at this same school.) The following fall (1913), Ruth taught grades one through nine at the Huscher School (District 57), a total of 34 students. She then taught 23 students at District 61, the "Woodruff School," founded and run by her uncle David. She finished at District 48 (Sulphur Springs/Aurora Township) with 18 students in her class.

Ruth was the eldest child in the family. She was strong and healthy. She was also good with horses. The family remembers a story about a horse she had partially broken in named Brownie.

While teaching, Ruth would go to school in a wagon pulled by Brownie. Every morning, her brothers would hitch Brownie to the wagon. Ruth would climb in; then the boys would point the wagon

---

[48] Cesil, Cora, Fannie, Grace, Harold, Lena, Pearl, and Ruth. Esther received her teaching certificate, but whether she took a teaching position cannot be verified.

in the direction of the school and let go. The horse would run all the way to the schoolhouse; Ruth would stop by running him into a fence. The boys in her class would come out, hold the reins so she could get out, then unhitch the horse and tether him for the day. Then, after school, the sequence was reversed for her trip home.[49]

Cesil followed in her older sister's footsteps. Graduating from the same normal college class, she taught at District 7 school right after Ruth. She continued teaching for many years, including in District 23 (Heber), District 34 (Grant), District 47 (Concordia), and Districts 48 and 89 (Sulphur Springs/Aurora), as well as in Glasco. The county was greatly indebted to the efforts of these two young ladies.

Cesil was less than five feet tall. Her uncle Ulysses Travis used to tease her gently about her height. Despite this, she could be a commanding presence in the classroom when she wanted to be.

Grace Woodruff taught for a number of years in virtually every corner of the county, beginning with District 1 (Shirley), District 8 (Lincoln), District 62 (Meredith), District 80 (Hollis), and District 81 (Summit).

Cora mainly worked in the northeastern townships. She taught at No. 1 (Shirley) and No. 15 (Elk).

Fannie was assigned to the eastern and northeastern portion, including District 15 (Cranmer), District 29 (Shirley), and District 71 (Colfax). She was regarded as an exemplary teacher. The local paper reported:

> *Miss Fannie Woodruff closed a very successful term of school at Cranmer Friday.... Miss Woodruff has given such good satisfaction that she has been given the school for the next year at a nice advance in salary.*[50]

---

49 Her sister Cesil would also use Brownie when she became a teacher. But he was much calmer and easier to manage after training with Ruth for a year.

50 *Clyde Voice-Republican*, Clyde, Kansas, 29 April 1918, page 17, column 6.

After graduating from Clyde High School, Lena remained loyal to her town, teaching in the Clyde public school system for many years.

Harold Woodruff taught briefly at District 91 (Starr) in 1916. The previous year, his sister Grace had been unable to teach due to the mumps. Harold walked every day from his home in Concordia to District 81 in Summit to substitute for her until she recovered.

Esther was educated at normal nollege, but there is no record of her ever having taught in the Cloud County school system.

Left: Cesil Woodruff. Right: Ruth Woodruff. Graduation photo, 1911.

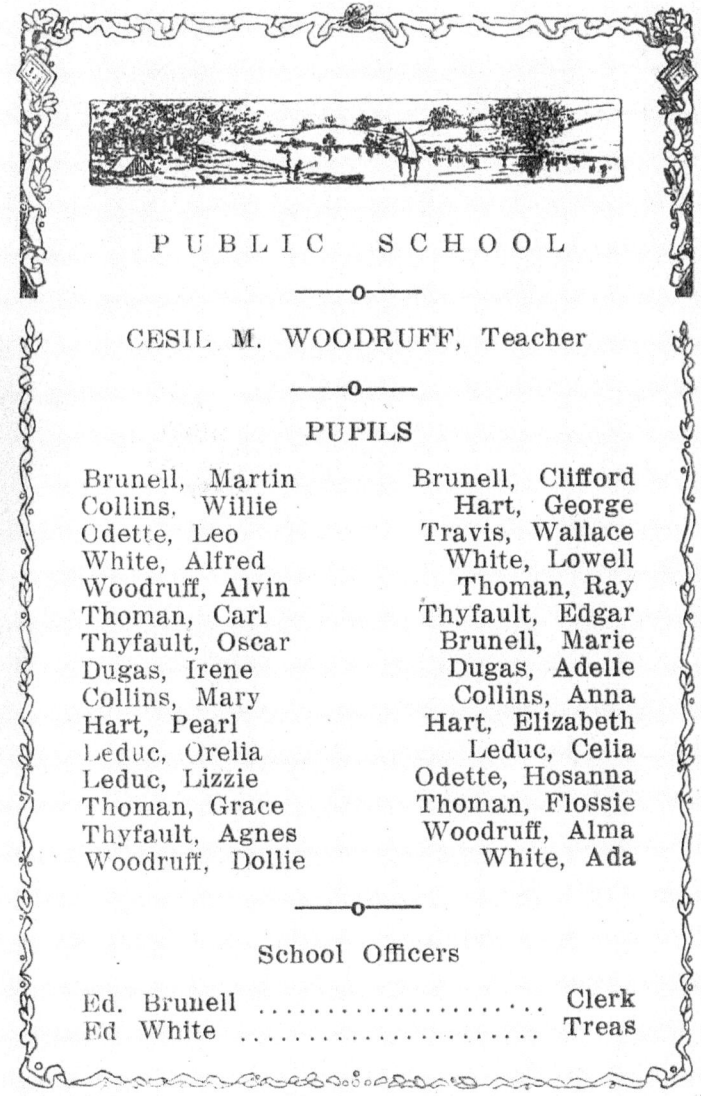

PUBLIC SCHOOL

CESIL M. WOODRUFF, Teacher

PUPILS

Brunell, Martin
Collins, Willie
Odette, Leo
White, Alfred
Woodruff, Alvin
Thoman, Carl
Thyfault, Oscar
Dugas, Irene
Collins, Mary
Hart, Pearl
Leduc, Orelia
Leduc, Lizzie
Thoman, Grace
Thyfault, Agnes
Woodruff, Dollie

Brunell, Clifford
Hart, George
Travis, Wallace
White, Lowell
Thoman, Ray
Thyfault, Edgar
Brunell, Marie
Dugas, Adelle
Collins, Anna
Hart, Elizabeth
Leduc, Celia
Odette, Hosanna
Thoman, Flossie
Woodruff, Alma
White, Ada

School Officers

Ed. Brunell .... Clerk
Ed White .... Treas

1916 School souvenir given by Cesil Woodruff to her students. Note that two of her sisters are pupils in her class.

Woodruff children at Nelson School, District 86 in 1910.
All seven of Isaac Woodruff's children are in the class
(Alma, Alvin, Cesil, Dorothea, Joseph, Ruth, Timothy.)

Souvenir from Dist. 84 School (Sulphur Springs) in Aurora. Siblings Alma, Alvin, Dolly and Joseph Woodruff listed as pupils.

Public Service

Some of the family again ventured into public affairs, though not as prominently as David Woodruff had. Isaac Woodruff served as juror for the county. He also served as local delegate for the Chicago Republican convention. Edmond Woodruff served as counting clerk for the local election, as well as presidential elector for the Prohibition Party.

Mechanics and Racing

George Woodruff began a new career. He left the telephone company and began repairing engines around the county, becoming an auto mechanic. Two years later, he added race car driving to his talents, competing as far away as Kansas City and Missouri. He often drove a Buick Model 19. His first competition was at the Belleville Auto Race, where he placed second, beating many seasoned professionals.

Later, he nearly won another race but snapped an axle, losing a wheel that flew into the crowd, injuring one of the spectators. George's car plowed up the track for about 50 feet, but he maintained control. He managed to finish in third place. He continued racing for several years, often as the winning driver.

He was quite an accomplished mechanic. He built a race car from the ground up, using parts from four different car models and getting them all to fit and work together.

In 1912 he and a partner started a shop specializing in auto storage and maintenance. Two years later he purchased a half-interest in an automobile repair shop. "Peebles and Woodruff" was a respected establishment, eventually moving into the giant Buick dealership complex in Concordia

> Otto Wilcox   J. W. Burnside
>
> ## The Wilcox=Burnside
> # GARAGE
>
> . . .Agents for Ford Cars. . .
>
> We have fine facilities for storing and caring for your car during the winter months. We sell all supplies for the Ford cars, also general supplies and accessories for all automobiles. This is the agency for Federal and G. & J. tires — none better make. Buy your gasoline, lubricating oils, and make your presto-lite tank exchanges here.
>
> ### Campbell & Woodruff
>
> Have full control and charge of the repair department of this garage, where all class of repair work will be done in a workmanlike manner and at a reasonable charge.
>
> ### Give us a Trial.

1912 advertisement, George Woodruff's garage.

> ## Auto Repairing.
>
> It is a saving of money to run your car into the garage when you first detect something not working right—it doesn't pay to put it off until the next day.
>
> We are auto doctors and there are few troubles that we cannot alleviate. Our charges are reasonable, our work the best and we can "FIXIT" right away.
>
> You can telephone us either phone 63
>
> Carbon Removed In Thirty Minutes
>
> ## Peebles & Woodruff
> ON BROADWAY

1915 advertisement, George Woodruff's auto repair shop.

He drove on the Kansas White Way,[51] which opened in 1914; it was the forerunner of the famous Route 66, built 12 years later. Roads between towns in those days were poor quality—unpaved and muddy. The White Way was an effort to develop an improved east-west highway to connect towns and increase commerce and tourism. The *Concordia Blade-Empire* reported:

> *The Kansas White Way is the most direct, the best and most practical route across the state of Kansas. It is the logical link in a great national transcontinental highway.*[52]

Delegates from 10 different Kansas counties met; together they selected a route for what they called "one of the greatest highways in the state."

Public support for the route was incredibly enthusiastic. Virtually every newspaper in the county carried front-page accounts, announcing developments and progress. Over several months, thousands of articles were published. The campaign got the route included in the 1914 Blue Book.[53]

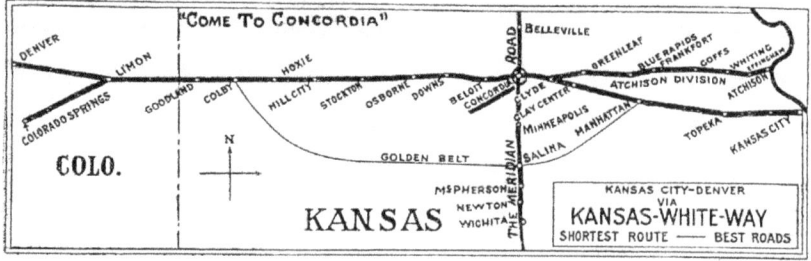

Map of the Kansas White Way 10 August 1914

---

51 Now Kansas Highway 9.

52 "Kansas White Way," *Concordia Blade-Empire*, Concordia, Kansas, 10 August 1914, page 3, column 4.

53 Automobile Blue Book. A touring handbook of the main automobile routes in the western United States.

George and wife Beulah moved to Idaho in January 1918, then on to Riverside, California, by 1920. There, George worked as a mechanic until he died on 5 June 1923.

Professional Sports

Even in professional sports, the Woodruff family made their mark. Charles Woodruff was a star halfback for the Clyde football team, considered one of the best in the state at the time. They were unbeaten in his senior year.

After graduation, he went on to play for the Clyde city team, which joined the American Legion Football League.[54]

1905 Clyde High School Football team including Charles Woodruff.

---

54 An early forerunner of the National Football League.

Community/Church Organizations

Several family members were prominent in various organizations, particularly musical, religious or fraternal ones.

Religion was an important part of everyday life. Edmond not only sang at the Methodist church but managed the choir as well. He was also an officer in the Methodist Church Public Welfare League. His wife, Cora, was trustee of the church. Lena was the regular organist at the Presbyterian church, playing Clyde's famous pipe organ. Fannie was also a delegate to the state Presbyterian convention.

Edmond continued to pursue his love of music by directing the Clyde town choir as well.[55]

The family was also involved in Masonic affairs. Edmond held several senior offices in the local lodge, including senior warden, senior deacon, and local delegate to the Masonic Grand Lodge. Pearl devoted her energies to the Rebekahs, the female branch of the Masons; she held several offices, including vice grand, and was a delegate to the Rebekah Grand Lodge in Wichita. She was also a member of the Order of the Eastern Star.[56]

Beneficial activities extended even to farming; Hiram was vice president in Colfax for the organization to control hog cholera.[57]

Farming

Since the early 1870s, there had always been Woodruffs working the land. While many family members had turned to other livelihoods, some were still engaged in farming. Arthur, Clark, Isaac, and Charles owned and operated their own farms; Lewis worked as a farm laborer. Harold taught school and also labored on the farms.

---

[55] Eventually elected president of the town choir.

[56] A charitable organization to provide welfare for relatives of Master Masons. It was devoted to religious, charitable, and educational purposes.

[57] Also known as swine fever. A highly contagious disease affecting swine, sometimes approaching 100 percent mortality.

In 1916, Harold, Hiram, and Albert ran a threshing operation for the area farmers, sometimes traveling as far as Alton, Kansas (100 miles away).

Roads

Roads were primitive at best. Inside town limits, only some roads were paved. Outside the townships, none were.

On sunny days, travel involved a bumpy, dusty ride. And when it rained, the roads turned into muddy quagmires. Cars and wagons plowed deep ruts; as the mud dried, the ruts remained, making the way unusable.

More than once, Grace was unable to return home after teaching school in Aurora because the roads were impassable. Edmond would sometimes do the rounds on his mail route and travel between towns on horseback; the road conditions made it impossible to travel any other way.

Such roads required frequent maintenance.

Arthur Woodruff, among others, shouldered the duty of dragging the roads. Under average conditions, a man could drag one mile of road in three hours, or roughly three miles per day.[58] This was not a glamorous job; it was hard, tiring, tedious work. But Arthur helped keep the county's arteries open for the citizens of his township.

---

58 US Department of Agriculture, Office of Public Roads and Rural Engineering, *Farmer's Bulletin* 597, "The Road Drag and How it is Used," revised March 1917.

Dragging the muddy dirt roads between farms.

World War I

Since 1914, most of the world had been embroiled in what was then the deadliest military conflict in history, "the war to end all wars."

For three years, the United States had remained neutral.

Suddenly, in November 1917, America entered the war, and life suddenly and drastically changed. Every corner of the nation was affected; Cloud County was no exception. Normal routines were replaced by wartime priorities. The Selective Service conscripted men into the armed forces. Goods were diverted to the war effort; there were shortages and rationing.

When the US entered the conflict, Kansas had a population of 1.7 million; eighty thousand Kansans served in the armed forces. Cloud County at that time only had eighteen thousand residents—approximately one percent of the state's population. Yet those in the county still contributed their share; dozens enlisted and served.

Woodruff family members contributed more than their fair share. Many were listed in the Selective Service draft (Albert, Arthur, Charles, George, Harold, Hiram, Julius and Joseph Woodruff). Most of these enlisted voluntarily before they were conscripted. Joseph and Hiram were called up to serve. Hiram, employed as a mailing clerk at the time, enlisted in the Navy and was assigned to the Supply Service. Harold entered the radio department and trained as an electrical engineer. He was assigned to the signal corps and served in France. Cousins Hiram and Albert led the camp in firearms use, posting the class's two highest shooting scores (Albert scored eight bullseyes out of 10 shots with a .45 caliber pistol; Hiram hit 2 out of five).

The community supported the local boys who served. When the recruits departed for camp, there was almost a holiday atmosphere. When Hiram left (along with 66 other recruits), for example, a parade was held, including the State Guard and the Grand Army of the Republic (a veterans' organization). An estimated two thousand people turned up at the Union Pacific train station to see them off.

Of all the Woodruffs, Albert's contribution was by far the most remarkable, and not just because of his marksmanship. In normal college, he was an exceptional student. He was president of the mathematics club, member of the debate team and a reporter for the Delphian literary society. Newspapers praised his oration skills; in the 1916 Republican Mock Convention, he led the Indiana delegation and delivered one of the most powerful speeches of the day. He graduated as the top mathematics and science student in his class and planned on pursuing mathematics and science degrees at the University of Iowa.

In college, Albert earned a reputation for dignity and did not pay much attention to girls. Friends hinted that he was afraid of them; Albert replied he was simply too busy with studies and did not have the time.

His doubters were proved wrong in Albert's senior year. The normal college held a fundraising event for the YWCA. A local movie theater agreed to donate half the proceeds of one night to the charity. A girl approached Albert to purchase a ticket; he refused, saying "I don't care to go alone and I haven't the time to make a date." She asked if he would buy some tickets if she got him a date. He jokingly replied, "I'll take ten if you can find the girls." She found ten girls to go out with him. The group of eleven, plus a chaperone, went to see a Mary Pickford film.

The usher was quite rattled when the procession arrived, exclaiming "he must be a cousin of the Sultan of Turkey." The entire theater broke into applause as they were escorted to their seats. The girls had a wonderful time. Albert bought them snacks during the show and took them all to a refreshment parlor before seeing them home. The girls said he was a perfect gentleman, and that they "Just had a grand time."

After the US entered the war, he enlisted in the Signal Corps. He was sent to officer's school, eventually becoming a second lieutenant. He was reassigned as an instructor at Fort Leavenworth, teaching mathematics and aviation; those who passed his classes went on to become aviation officers in the war.

Albert Woodruff, 1918

Harold Woodruff, 1919.

Contributions were not limited to the battlefield. Like most Americans of the time, Woodruffs acted in support roles. As a teacher, Fannie raised funds for the Junior Red Cross effort. Maude sold War Savings Stamps. Edmond used his mail route to drum up business, selling hundreds of war bonds to finance the war effort. Hazel trained as an ambulance driver for the battle theater.[59] Many of the wives contributed baked goods for sales to help pay for needed goods and services.

Thankfully, none of the Woodruffs perished. When the war ended the following year, all returned home safely.

Spanish Flu

By 1918, the deadliest war in modern history was drawing to a close. By the time it ended, around 17 million had perished in the conflict. Fortune had smiled on the Woodruffs, who had not lost a single family member in the war. They, along with the rest of the community, were looking forward to returning to a normal life.

Then, on the heels of what was then the bloodiest war in history, came the deadliest disease since the Black Plague. Over a span of only two years, between 50 million and 100 million people died. The United States alone suffered over 675,000 deaths—more than it had in World War I, World War II, the Korean War, and the Vietnam War combined.

The name "Spanish flu" is a misnomer. Most historians now believe that the epidemic originated on a pig farm in Haskell County, Kansas. The rapid influx of soldiers for training carried it to Camp Funston, just north of Concordia. On 4 March 1918, the first official death was recorded—that of Albert Gitchell, an army cook at Camp Funston. Once in the camp, the flu quickly spread through the ranks, then worldwide as the troops deployed.

---

59 She lived in Idaho at the time.

There seemed to be no safe haven from this epidemic. Because viruses had not yet been discovered, the flu appeared to strike suddenly and without cause. Unlike other diseases, it attacked younger, healthier individuals, often killing in a matter of days or sometimes even hours.

Cloud County (literally "ground zero" of the pandemic) keenly felt the impact. Many citizens fell ill, including Woodruffs. Charles, Edmond, Grace, and George all contracted the virus. Fortunately, all four survived. The disease was so pervasive that quarantines were imposed; no public gatherings were allowed. Edmond's choir was forbidden to practice or perform until the quarantine was lifted. Grace fell severely ill from the flu in December 1918. It took her nearly one month to recover, as she had also contracted pneumonia.

Illnesses and Deaths

Aside from the Spanish flu, other diseases and afflictions also seriously affected the community, including the Woodruffs.

Many tools of modern medicine did not exist. Penicillin was not available until 1928. Injury, illness, and death were a part of everyday life of the time. Woodruffs were not immune to this.

In the 1910s, the most prominent loss was the death of David Woodruff in 1914. But other family deaths were no less devastating.

In 1911, Isaac's 14-year-old son, Timothy, died of diabetes. This was the second child Isaac and wife Mary Elizabeth had lost to this disease; the first was their eldest child, Ova, a dozen years before. Timothy was buried in Nelson Cemetery.

Three years later, Mary Elizabeth herself died suddenly. She would often get severe headaches and used a belt or kerchief tied very tight to help the pain. One morning she woke up, tied a rope around her head, and proceeded to do the day's chores. She heated water, did the washing by hand, and hung it out to dry. Then she made bread and some pumpkin pies.⁶⁰ She prepared supper and then took a dose of the belladonna medicine prescribed by her doctor. She then said she felt funny and went to lie down for a few minutes. The family thought she was asleep, but she had died. The official cause of death was listed as uremic poisoning and a drug overdose.⁶¹ She died on 2 April 1916—at only 50 years old—and was buried in Nelson Cemetery.

At the time, both Ruth and Cesil were busy administering school examinations. They each received an urgent telephone call to return home. They both knew something bad had happened and were sure that someone had died. When Ruth arrived at the house, her father came outside. Then she knew that it was her mother who had passed. All the children were devastated. Even Ruth's brother-in-law, the Reverend Ulysses G. Travis, was called away from his duties to attend to the tragedy.

Mary Elizabeth's obituary was printed by no less than eight of the local papers, from Concordia to Miltonvale to Belleville, devoting large amounts of space to describing what a kind, wonderful person she was.⁶² One of her obituaries read:

> *Mary L. Jennings... lived a true Christian life, she was a loving wife and mother and devoted her life in helping others, always thinking of others rather than herself. She will be missed from the community and by a host of friends.*⁶³

Emmette Woodruff was also officially declared dead in 1916, although by this time, the news was hardly a shock to the community. He had disappeared on 14 April 1909. He was never heard from again. His wife, Ruby, obtained a divorce in 1911 on the grounds of abandonment, but Emmette could not be declared dead until seven

---

60 She told Isaac they were sweet potato pies; he always said pumpkins were only fit for pigs. But he couldn't tell the difference on his own.

61 This gave Cesil a lifelong distrust of doctors.

62 By contrast, when Isaac passed away several years later, only two papers noted his death, and that was with one short paragraph each.

63 *Concordia Blade-Empire*, Concordia, Kansas, 11 April 1916, page 2, column 1.

years after he was last seen. Brother Edmond became the guardian of Emmette's daughters in the interim.

This caused legal complications when his father, David, died three years after the disappearance, as Emmette was an heir but could not be contacted. The estate was tied up until Emmette was legally declared dead, and his stake passed on to his children. The estate administrator, Edmond Silas Woodruff, had to initiate a partition suit to dispose of David's estate, which included several homes and 567 acres of land in the county.

Injury and illness were no strangers to rural life. Broken bones, blood poisoning from cuts and infection, and other such injuries were common. But there were some more serious, longer-lasting events of note.

In 1912, Albert Woodruff's daughter Hildred fell from a horse and broke her upper arm an inch above the elbow. The doctors at Clay Center (Drs. F. A. McDonald and S. C. Pigman) reportedly set the bone improperly; afterwards, Hildred's arm became shortened and deformed. Albert filed a suit against the doctors for malpractice, asserting his daughter was permanently crippled and asking for up to $10,000 in damages. The case was eventually dismissed in district court.

The following year, Lewis's family was stricken with mumps; five family members contracted the disease. It was quite serious, as all were adults. Lewis's wife, Alice, became extremely ill as a result. Grace was unable to teach school. The entire family battled this for a couple weeks before they recovered. Fortunately, there were no deaths or permanent effects.

Anson was badly injured in the autumn of 1915 when horses pulling his wagon were spooked. Anson fell, hurting his head and spraining his back. For months afterwards, he could not walk.

Harold Woodruff, still teaching school near Miltonvale, dislocated both arms while working in the fields when a hay rack overturned on him.

Anson's son Silas had previously moved to Michigan and then Illinois. In 1917 he relocated to Panama City, Panama. Working as a fireman, he became a lieutenant in the force.

Marriages

While there was plenty of hardship, death, and suffering in the Woodruffs' daily lives, there were also reasons for joy. In these small towns, a marriage could be a source of happiness. And this was definitely the Woodruffs' decade for matrimony; a total of nine family members were married within seven years.

Locally, there were few social diversions available—no television or radio, and not even a phone in many homes. Entertainment could sometimes be found in Concordia, but for many, this was a long, arduous journey, to be undertaken only when necessary.

Thus, country weddings were a special cause for joy. They were doubly so for the Woodruffs, who frequently turned them into major social occasions for family and friends. It was not unheard of for 50 to one hundred guests to gather for a family wedding.

Family members who tied the knot in this decade:

1 October 1913: George Woodruff and Beulah Schraier

9 May 1915: Ruth Woodruff and Albert ("Bert") Johnson

14 February 1917: Pearl Woodruff and Harrison Chesebro

22 November 1917: Charles Woodruff and Myrna Christian

31 December 1917: Hiram Woodruff and Aura Birch

27 September 1918: Dollie Woodruff and Moses Will; Joseph Woodruff and Jenny Will[64]

23 May 1919: Cora May Woodruff and Amaziah ("Maizie") Smith

---

64 Dollie's brother Joseph married Moses's sister Jenny. The couples were married at the same time in a double ceremony.

11 September 1919: Lena Woodruff and Leslie Gerhardt

1915 Wedding photo, Ruth Woodruff and Albert Johnson.

Wedding photo, Moses Elias Will and Dorothea "Dolly" Will. 1918.

Miscellaneous Events

A few other events are worth noting here.

Lewis and his wife, Alice, moved to Idaho in 1917. They took their two youngest, Naomi and James, with them, while the older children remained in Cloud County. Cora stayed with Aunt Jessie and Uncle Ulysses G. Travis. Harold boarded with another farm family. Grace, unmarried and teaching school, lived independently. Two years later, Lewis and his family decided to return to Cloud County. Daughter Grace purchased a farm near Cranmer (the Nelse Bottger farm) for her parents to live on when they arrived.[65]

Isaac Woodruff, along with daughter Ruth and "Bert" Johnson, drove from Aurora to Kirksville, Missouri, in the family's Model T Ford touring car and returned home the same day—over six hundred miles round trip.[66] Given the primitive road conditions—and the fact that the Model T's top speed was about 40 miles per hour—this was a remarkable achievement.

In 1919, Edmond Silas Woodruff—a pillar of the community—was arrested and charged with discharging a gun within Clyde city limits. Spectators filled the building to witness the trial. The case took all afternoon, and nearly 40 witnesses were summoned to the stand. Edmond was found guilty and fined $25 plus court costs.[67]

---

65 "Hollis," *Concordia Blade-Empire*, Concordia, Kansas, 30 June 1919, page 5, column 2.
66 *Miltonvale Record*, 29 August 1918, page 4, column 4.
67 "Found Guilty," *Clyde Voice-Republican*, Clyde, Kansas, 15 May 1919, page 1, column 4.

Woodruffs had impacted so much of everyday life by now, including in farming, education, business, and government. There was no question of their influence, both direct and indirect, over the years.

But their chapter in Cloud County was drawing to a close.

8
1920s: Departure

The Roaring Twenties were years of Prohibition and speakeasies. The country now had a hundred million people for the first time. The League of Nations was established. Women secured the right to vote with the 19th Amendment. The construction of Yankee Stadium began.

The entertainment age was beginning. The NBC Radio Network was born, opening 24 stations. Television was invented two years later. A pair of famous performers—Mickey and Minnie Mouse—made their debut on the silver screen.

The year 1926 saw the most snowfall in recorded history for Cloud County within 24 hours (14 inches). Aurora approved bonds for a water system with two wells; the town was now at the height of its prosperity, with 36 businesses.

The county also proudly entered the modern age. The Kansas-Nebraska Radio Club (KNRC) was established. Charlie Bosser purchased land to establish the first airport in the region.

From the time Hiram, David, and Anson first arrived in 1871 until 1919, there had been nearly one hundred Woodruffs in the region. But the family's star was waning; when the Roaring Twenties began, only half of this number remained. By 1930, only 28 were left.

Albert E. Woodruff moved his large family to Arizona prior to 1920, then relocated to Riverside, California, 10 years later. William left for Ohio. Della, who remained in the area, died in 1922. Lena departed for Cedar Rapids. Esther, working as a local restaurant cook, left in August 1920 to join her parents in Boise, Idaho.

Albert Woodruff, Lewis Woodruff's son, completed his Master of Science degree at the University of Chicago, and became professor of Physics at Butler University in Indianapolis.

Clark Woodruff, living on his father David's original homestead, was clerk of District 61 school (Woodruff school).

Some family members remained in Cloud County. Arthur continued dragging the roads, keeping them clear and usable. On the whole, they appeared to live quiet lives. Aside from an occasional marriage or special event, there is little mention of them in the newspapers after 1925.

Julius Woodruff and his cousin William Mottin opened a machine shop north of Miltonvale, including automotive engine repairs. He also was appointed mail carrier for RFD Route 4, continuing the Woodruff postal tradition.

Maude Woodruff became a teacher in the county district schools, continuing the Woodruff tradition. Beulah Woodruff continued to enrich the community by teaching piano, just as her aunt Lena had done years before. Charles Woodruff engaged in farming; he advertised purebred horses for breeding.

8
1920s: Departure

The Roaring Twenties were years of Prohibition and speakeasies. The country now had a hundred million people for the first time. The League of Nations was established. Women secured the right to vote with the 19th Amendment. The construction of Yankee Stadium began.

The entertainment age was beginning. The NBC Radio Network was born, opening 24 stations. Television was invented two years later. A pair of famous performers—Mickey and Minnie Mouse—made their debut on the silver screen.

The year 1926 saw the most snowfall in recorded history for Cloud County within 24 hours (14 inches). Aurora approved bonds for a water system with two wells; the town was now at the height of its prosperity, with 36 businesses.

The county also proudly entered the modern age. The Kansas-Nebraska Radio Club (KNRC) was established. Charlie Bosser purchased land to establish the first airport in the region.

From the time Hiram, David, and Anson first arrived in 1871 until 1919, there had been nearly one hundred Woodruffs in the region. But the family's star was waning; when the Roaring Twenties began, only half of this number remained. By 1930, only 28 were left.

Albert E. Woodruff moved his large family to Arizona prior to 1920, then relocated to Riverside, California, 10 years later. William left for Ohio. Della, who remained in the area, died in 1922. Lena departed for Cedar Rapids. Esther, working as a local restaurant cook, left in August 1920 to join her parents in Boise, Idaho.

Albert Woodruff, Lewis Woodruff's son, completed his Master of Science degree at the University of Chicago, and became professor of Physics at Butler University in Indianapolis.

Clark Woodruff, living on his father David's original homestead, was clerk of District 61 school (Woodruff school).

Some family members remained in Cloud County. Arthur continued dragging the roads, keeping them clear and usable. On the whole, they appeared to live quiet lives. Aside from an occasional marriage or special event, there is little mention of them in the newspapers after 1925.

Julius Woodruff and his cousin William Mottin opened a machine shop north of Miltonvale, including automotive engine repairs. He also was appointed mail carrier for RFD Route 4, continuing the Woodruff postal tradition.

Maude Woodruff became a teacher in the county district schools, continuing the Woodruff tradition. Beulah Woodruff continued to enrich the community by teaching piano, just as her aunt Lena had done years before. Charles Woodruff engaged in farming; he advertised purebred horses for breeding.

Isaac Woodruff had moved to California 20 years earlier, then returned to Cloud County after only a couple years. Now, he moved back to the Golden State, this time to Pasadena. With him went one daughter, Ruth; her husband, Albert Johnson; and their family. Cesil, who was unmarried, did not accompany them.

Cesil did not like her father but was brought up to honor and respect her parents. From the money she had saved, she bought him a home in Pasadena with two bedrooms. The second bedroom was reserved for her so she could visit him. The house was placed in Isaac's name.

The first time she visited, she was shocked to find that he had remarried. His new wife, Ella Peale, was a widow with two daughters. She left one child at a private orphanage and moved the other into the bedroom Cesil had reserved for herself. Cesil was livid.

Isaac died in 1925 of stomach cancer. He had previously transferred the Kansas farm to Cesil, in return for "Ten Dollars and [ironically for him] Love and Affection." In his will, he left the Pasadena house and his bank accounts to his new wife; to his children he left the Kansas property, to be divided between them.

Cesil traveled to California to transport Isaac's body back to Kansas. He is buried in Nelson Cemetery, beside his first wife, Mary Elizabeth, the children's beloved mother. She, sister Alma, Dorothea and husband Moses Will, and Joseph with wife Jenny Will, all relocated to California over the next few years.

The last known Woodruff in the area, Robert Wayne Woodruff, died in 2010; he is now buried in Miltonvale Cemetery. As of this writing, there are no residents in Cloud County with this surname. It is likely that some family members still reside there but have different surnames through marriage.

Nothing is left on the original homesteads of David and Hiram. David's homestead is now owned by a commercial farming company, and all the buildings have been taken down. Hiram's property is still inhabited, but all buildings now standing were built after 1910, well after he sold it and had moved to California.[68]

Once large and influential, the family's presence is gone; they are only mentioned in passing in history texts or found in the cemetery records. Soon their memory may fade forever.

Or perhaps not.

Over a century after Hiram's departure, the current owner of the homestead commented, "I remember a Woodruff used to own this place. He had a brother with a farm nearby, didn't he?" Several others also remember the Woodruff School. Some remember where it stood for decades.

The Woodruffs' many achievements helped Cloud County grow through its early years and mold it into the community it is today. Those living there now can thank them for their hard work and contributions. And descendants of the Woodruff brothers can be proud of their heritage.

---

[68] These might have been built by Clark Woodruff, who took ownership of the farm in 1903 after Hiram left for California.

AUCTION!
FOR
Isaac Woodruff

4 MILES SOUTH OF AURORA, 16 MILES EAST AND 2 NORTH OF
GLASCO AND 5 MILES WEST AND 3 NORTH OF MILTONVALE.

Wed.   Oct.   6th.

BEGINNING AT 11 O'CLOCK   LANOUE & LECLAIR'S LUNCH
Everything must sell as I am going to California

5 Horses and Mules 5

1 black mare, 8 yrs. old, weight 1400   1 black mare colt 2 yrs. old
1 brown mare, 8 yrs. old, .. 1400   1 molly mule, 1 yr. old. 1 colt 2 yrs. old

24 Head of Cattle 24

4 good milk cows, 5 & 7 yrs. old   5 steers long yearlings
3 yearlings heifers   3 2 yrs. old heifers coming fresh
1 Red Poll bull calf, 6 weeks old   2 Red Poll heifers, 8 months old
1 Holstein Pure Bred heifer, 4 mos. old 5 spring calves

1 sow and 5 pigs   5 shoats, weighing 75 pounds

1 stand of bees.   60 Rhode Island Red hens.   75 or 80 spring chickens

Implements & Feed

1 new Winona wagon. 1 Bane wagon. 1 rack & wagon. 1 top buggy. 1 road cart 1 McCormick 7 foot good binder. 1 Deering mower new. 1 Dandy cultivator. 1 Ohio cultivator. 1 hay rake. 1 row weed cutter. 1-14 in. walking plow new. 1-3 section harrow. 1 riding lister. 12 rods of hog wire. 1 sulky plow. 1 grinder. 1 scoop board. 1 sled. 1 rack. 1 saddle. 1-12 hole Press drill new. 1 disk harrow. 1 grindstone. 1 cider mill. 12 feet of log chain. 75 feet of galvanized pipe. 2 sets of work harness. 2 sets of single buggy harness. 1 fly net single 1 hand cornplanter. 1 Ford Touring car 1916 Model in good order. 1 cross cut saw. 1 post augur, 1 sledge hammar. 1 hay knife. 1 big plow umbrella. 1-50 gals galvanized oil tank. 5 tons of millet and alfalfa in stack. 12 tons of alfalfa in barn. straw from 500 bus. of oats. 6 acres of corn in field.

Household Goods

3 beds & springs. 1 sanitary cot. 1 mattress. 2 dressers. 1 kitchen table. 2-4 hole oil stoves. 1 oil heater. 1 coal & wood heater. 1 wood heater. 1 cast iron range. 1 American cream separator 600 cap. 9 dining room chairs 4 rocking chairs. 1-20 gal jar, 1 high chair, 1 go-cart. 1 kitchen cabinet. 1 wash stand 1 2½ H. P. engine & washing machine. 1-10 gal jar. 6 or 8 dozs fruit jars. 1 ice cream freezer. 1 ironing board. 3 milk cans 15 & 10 gals.   Other articles too numerous to mention.

TERMS: Sums of $10.00 and under cash. On sums over this amount asmt credit of 12 months time will be given on bankable note bearing 8 per cent interest.   No property removed until settled for.

Floyd McCall   **Elwood Bros.**
CLERK   AUCTIONEERS

Auction, Isaac Woodruff's farm. *Aurora Searchlight*, 23 September 1923.

1889. Albert E. Woodruff, wife Carrie Huscher and daughter Ada Maude Woodruff.

BIBLIOGRAPHY

Books and Publications

Andrews, M. R. (1902). *History of Marietta and Washington County, Ohio.* Chicago: Biographical Publishing Company.

Blackmar, F., ed. (1912). *Kansas: A Cyclopedia of State History, Embracing Events, Institutions, Industries, Counties, Cities, Towns, Prominent Persons, etc. ...* vol. 1. Chicago: Standard Publishing Company.

Brown, C. (1902). *Southampton, Long Island, NY, History: The History of Long Island from Its Earliest Settlement to the Present Time.* New York: Lewis Publishing Company.

Cloud County History (1992). Concordia: Cloud County Historical Society, Concordia, Kansas.

Coon, P. R. (2009). *Spirit and Times of Evelyn Alice Johnson Colvin: Memories and Family History.* Privately published.

Cowper, J. M. (1892). *Canterbury Marriage Licenses, First Series, 1568–1618.* Canterbury: Cross and Jackman.

Cowper, J. M. (1894). *Canterbury Marriage Licenses, Second Series, 1619–1660.* Canterbury: Cross and Jackman.

Cutler, W. G. (1883). *History of the State of Kansas.* Chicago: A. T. Andreas.

Emery, J. P. (1970). *It Takes People to Make a Town: The Story of Concordia, Kansas, 1871–1971.* Arrow Print Co.

Flower, W. E. (1881). *Visitation of Yorkshire in the Years 1563 and 1564.* London: Mitchell and Hughes.

Hatfield, R. E. (1848). *History of Elizabeth, New Jersey; Including the Early History of Union County*. New York: Carlton & Lanahan.

Hedges, H., W. Pelletreau, and E. Foster (1874). *Book of Records of the Town of Southampton with Other Ancient Documents of Historic Value*. Sag Harbor, NY: John H. Hunt, Book and Job Printer.

Howell, G. R. (1866). *Early History of Southampton, L. I. New York, with Genealogies*. New York: J. N. Hallock, James Miller's Bookstore.

Hunter, J. R. (1831). *South Yorkshire and the History and Topography of the Deanery of Doncaster*. London: J. B. Nichols and Son.

Little, J. (1852). *Family Records or Genealogies of the First Settlers of Passaic Valley (and Vicinity) Above Chatham*. Feltfille, NJ: Stationers' Hall Press.

Meinig, D. W. (1993). *The Shaping of America: A Geographical Perspective on 500 Years of History*, vol. 2, *Continental America, 1800–1867*. New Haven: Yale University Press.

Palmer, F., and K. Chilen (1982). *Miltonvale—1982*. Miltonvale, Kansas.

Sheppard, A. L. (n.d.). "Woodruff Family History." Unpublished manuscript.

Torrey, C. A. (1985). *New England Marriages Prior to 1700*. Baltimore: Genealogical Publishing Co., Inc.

Woodruff, C., and M. R. Herod (1971). *Woodruff Chronicles, a Genealogy*, vol. 2. Glendale: Arthur H. Clark Company.

Woodruff, C. E. (1895). *History of the Town and Port of Fordwich*. Canterbury, Kent, UK: Cross & Jackman.

Woodruff, F. E. (1902). *A Branch of the Woodruff Stock*. Morristown, NJ: The Jerseyman.

Woodruff, F. E. (1909). *The Woodruffs of New Jersey*. New York: Grafton Press.

Woodruff, S. A. (1945). *A Branch of the Woodruff Family, 1640–1945: From John Woodruffe, the Younger John, Nathaniel Woodruff, and Stephen Woodruff of Southampton, L. I.* New York and Chicago.

Newspapers

(Years indicate timeframe of articles reviewed in each publication.)

Abilene Daily Reflector, Abilene, Kansas, 1919

Alliant, Concordia, Kansas, 1890–1893

BIBLIOGRAPHY

Aurora News, Aurora, Kansas, 1893

Aurora Searchlight, Aurora, Kansas, 1920

Blade and Empire, Concordia, Kansas 1902–1904

Cline's Press, Clyde, Kansas, 1884

Cloud County Blade, Concordia, Kansas, 1881

Cloud County Critic, Concordia, Kansas, 1882–1886

Clyde Argus, Clyde, Kansas, 1885–1895

Clyde Daily Republican, Clyde, Kansas, 1907

Clyde Democrat, Clyde, Kansas, 1880–1881

Clyde Herald, Clyde, Kansas, 1882–1906

Clyde Mail (Clyde Argus), Clyde, Kansas, 1887

Clyde Republican, Clyde, Kansas, 1901–1918

Clyde Voice-Republican, Clyde, Kansas, 1902–1920

Concordia Blade, Concordia, Kansas, 1889–1901

Concordia Blade-Empire, Concordia, Kansas, 1907–1920

Concordia Daily Blade, Concordia, Kansas, 1887–1919

Concordia Daily Kansan, Concordia, Kansas, 1905–1919

Concordia Daily Mail, Concordia, Kansas, 1887

Concordia Daylight, Concordia Kansas, 1886–1899

Concordia Empire, Concordia, Kansas, 1871–1919

Concordia Expositor, Concordia, Kansas, 1879-1881

Concordia News, Concordia, Kansas, 1918–1920

Concordia Press, Concordia, Kansas, 1901–1920

Concordia Republican, Concordia Kansas, 1880–1881

Concordia Semi-Weekly Times, Concordia, Kansas, 1887

Concordia Times, Concordia, Kansas, 1884–1891

Concordia Weekly Daylight, Concordia, Kansas, 1887–1888

Concordia Weekly Expositor, Concordia, Kansas, 1877–1883

Daily Blade, Concordia, Kansas, 1902–1916

Daily Reporter, Concordia, Kansas, 1887

Daylight, Concordia, Kansas 1888

District School, Aurora, Kansas, 1894

Empire Daylight, Concordia, Kansas, 1900–1901

Farmer's Voice, Clyde, Kansas, 1892–1918

Glasco Sun, Glasco, Kansas 1888–1889

Glasco Tribune, Glasco, Kansas, 1881

High School Zephyr, Clyde, Kansas, 1905

Kansan, Jamestown, Kansas, 1883–1919

Kansan, Concordia, Kansas, 1895–1920

Kansas Blade, Concordia, Kansas, 1883–1887

Kansas Conference Reporter, Clyde, Kansas, 1897–1898

Kansas Kritic, Concordia, Kansas, 1888

Kansas Optimist, Jamestown, Kansas, 1896–1918

Kansas Sunflower, Clyde, Kansas, 1898

Kansas Weekly Blade, Concordia, Kansas 1887–1888

Miltonvale Chieftain, Miltonvale, Kansas, 1888

Miltonvale News, Miltonvale, Kansas, 1883–1891

Miltonvale Press, Miltonvale, Kansas, 1892–1900

Miltonvale Record, Miltonvale, Kansas, 1901–1920

Miltonvale Review, Miltonvale, Kansas, 1889

Parsons Daily Republican, Parsons, Kansas, 1910

Press, Concordia, Kanas, 1901

Press, Miltonvale, Kansas, 1897

Quill, Jamestown, Kansas 1888-1889

Republic County Democrat, Belleville, Kansas, 1916

Republican Empire, Concordia, Kansas 1884–1885

Salina Semi-Weekly Journal, Salina, Kansas, 1912

Sun, Glasco, Kansas, 1883–1919

Voice-Republican, Clyde, Kansas, 1918

Weekly Daylight, Concordia, Kansas 1888-1889

Appendix A

Woodruff Teachers

It was once remarked that aside from being farmers, the Woodruffs were a family of teachers. And indeed, starting with David Woodruff, more than a dozen Woodruffs, through three generations, became certified and taught school in Cloud County and the area. For decades, Woodruffs could nearly always be found there as normal institute students. When the first professional institute was established, Woodruffs were in attendance. Many eventually moved to other states and established themselves as noteworthy educators.[69]

In light of this, it is interesting to note that the Woodruff children of this time appeared, as a rule, to be remarkably good students. Monthly school reports of the time frequently show Woodruff students with perfect attendance for the month, neither absent nor tardy. Several were near the top of their class or received awards for specific subjects.

Fannie Woodruff in particular was an exceptionally gifted student. While a senior in high school, she took the normal institute examination. 1500 students statewide took the exam; four students, Fannie among them, scored so highly that they were awarded an automatic two-year normal school teaching certificate. This

---

69 Many of their children also became teachers, but that is beyond the scope of this work.

automatically renewed every two years, in effect making it a lifetime teaching certificate.

Mary Elizabeth (Jennings) Woodruff had a bell she used when she taught school in the 1890s. This was given to her daughter, Ruth. The bell, along with a letter explaining its history, is given to a daughter or relative in the next generation who becomes a teacher. As of this writing, it has been handed down through five Woodruff generations. It is currently held by Ruth's great-granddaughter in Reno, Nevada.

The first three generations of Woodruffs produced the following teachers, who taught in nearly a third of the rural county schools. Together, they educated students in over three-quarters of the county townships.

The list below is of those who taught in Cloud County. Those known to have taught in other areas of the country have also been noted.

Albert Woodruff—District 23 (Heber), District 40 (Nelson), (US Army instructor during World War I, in mathematics and aviation); Professor of Physics, Butler University, Indianapolis, Indiana

Arthur Woodruff—unspecified school

Cesil Woodruff—District 23 (Heber), District 34 (Grant), District 47 (Concordia), District 48 (Sulphur Springs), District 84 (Sulphur Springs), District 89 (Sulphur Springs), Glasco; San Jacinto, California

Cora Woodruff—District 1 (Shirley), District 15 (Elk), District 21 (Valley), District 40 (Nelson)

David Woodruff—District 61 (Colfax—Woodruff School)

Fannie Woodruff—District 15 (Elk), District 29 (Shirley), District 71 (Carmel), Clyde public schools; Colorado, New Mexico

APPENDIX A

Grace Woodruff—District 1 (Shirley), District 8 (Lincoln), District 62 (Meredith), District 80 (Hollis), District 81 (Summit)

Harold Woodruff—District 36 (Colfax), District 91 (Starr), Hays.

Hazel Woodruff—Utah

Lena Woodruff—District 9 (Meredith), Clyde public schools

Mary Elizabeth (Jennings) Woodruff—District 57 (Huscher), District 61 (Colfax—Woodruff School), District 87 (Lincoln)

Mary Maude (McDonald) Woodruff—District 61 (Colfax—Woodruff School)

Mildred Genevieve Woodruff—unspecified school

Pearl Woodruff—unspecified school

Ruth Woodruff—District 7 (Heber), District 48 (Sulphur Springs), District 57 (Huscher), District 61 (Colfax—Woodruff School)

1903. Walter Campbell (son of Della Woodruff) with wife Lydia Bertrand. Wedding photo.

APPENDIX A

Grace Woodruff—District 1 (Shirley), District 8 (Lincoln), District 62 (Meredith), District 80 (Hollis), District 81 (Summit)

Harold Woodruff—District 36 (Colfax), District 91 (Starr), Hays.

Hazel Woodruff—Utah

Lena Woodruff—District 9 (Meredith), Clyde public schools

Mary Elizabeth (Jennings) Woodruff—District 57 (Huscher), District 61 (Colfax—Woodruff School), District 87 (Lincoln)

Mary Maude (McDonald) Woodruff—District 61 (Colfax—Woodruff School)

Mildred Genevieve Woodruff—unspecified school

Pearl Woodruff—unspecified school

Ruth Woodruff—District 7 (Heber), District 48 (Sulphur Springs), District 57 (Huscher), District 61 (Colfax—Woodruff School)

1903. Walter Campbell (son of Della Woodruff) with wife Lydia Bertrand. Wedding photo.

Appendix B

Woodruff Family Tree

Hiram Woodruff

Hiram Woodruff (b. 17 Oct 1835, d. 23 Jan 1904), m. 30 Sep 1857 Sarah Amanda Gilmore (b. 21 Apr 1840, d. 6 Apr 1925). Children:

1. *Della Woodruff (b. 16 Jul 1858, d. 12 Nov 1905), m. 28 Nov 1977 Joseph B. Campbell (b. 1854, d. 29 Jul 1923. Children:*
    a. Walter Hiram Campbell (b. 6 Oct 1878, d. 17 Nov 1960), m. 25 Mar 1903 Lydia Bertrand Campbell (b. 1 Jan 1881, d. 17 Jun 1968)
    b. Nellie Campbell (b. 7 Apr 1886), m. Lewis Trost (b. 1 Aug 1879, d. 8 Jan 1955)

2. *Florence Woodruff (b. 9 Mar 1860, d. 7 Mar 1909), m. 4 Apr 1896 James C. Fox (b. 1862)*

3. *Isaac Woodruff (b. 17 Jan 1862, d. 13 Feb 1925), m. (1) 19 Aug 1887 Mary Elizabeth Jennings (b. 18 Feb 1866, d. 2 Apr 1916), m. (2) circa Dec 1920 Sarah (Ella) E. Miller (b. 1873). Children from 1st marriage:*
    a. Ova M. Woodruff (b. 17 Sep 1888, d. 31 Dec 1898)
    b. Ruth Avonia Woodruff (b. 1 Oct 1894, d. 2 Feb 1973), m. (1) 9 May 1915 Albert Edward "Bert" Johnson (b. 20 Jun 1888, d. 15 Feb 1954), m. (2) 28 May 1932 Earl Edwin Johnson Darrow (b. 1903, d. 1978)

  c. Cesil Mae Woodruff (b. 30 Jan 1896, d. 19 Dec 1991), m. (1) 23 Jun 1927 James S. Pearson (b. 29 May 1888, d. 10 Oct 1971), m. (2) 3 Dec 1972 Dwight Badger Van Fleet (b. 26 Feb 1898, d. 15 Apr 1988)

  d. Timothy Woodruff (b. 10 Sep 1897, d. 27 Nov 1911)

  e. Joseph E. Woodruff (b. 13 Feb 1899, d. 20 Jan 1991), m. 27 Sep 1918 Jennie Katy Will (b. 13 Apr 1900, d. 18 Nov 1995)

  f. Dorothea (Dolly) Woodruff (b. 7 Jan 1901, d. 29 Jun 1968), m. 27 Sep 1918 Moses Elias Will (b. 7 Aug 1891, d. 16 Jun 1974)

  g. Alma Woodruff (b. 31 Jul 1903, d. 23 Nov 1963), m. 17 Jun 1926 Dwight Badger Van Fleet (b. 26 Feb 1898, d. 15 Apr 1988)

  h. Alvin John Woodruff (b. 31 Jul 1903, d. 29 Mar 1976), m. 14 Mar 1923 Dorothy Lower (b. 29 Nov 1904, d. 10 Feb 1993)

4. *Cora Woodruff (b. 23 Feb 1864, d. 31 Jan 1936), m. 30 Nov 1892 Thomas McClure (b. 1857, d. 1927) Children:*

  a. Irving Clay McClure (b. 9 Sep 1883, d. 6 Dec 1918), m. Vena Ruth Gage (9 Feb 1880, d. 17 Aug 1960)

  b. Harvey Russell McClure (b. 20 Aug 1890, d. 24 Dec 1961). Unmarried.

5. *Albert Ernest Woodruff (b. 20 Dec 1865, d. 18 Dec 1936), m. Oct 1888 Carrie Huscher (b. 18 Jun 1867, d. 1940) Children:*

  a. Ada Maude Woodruff (b. 4 May 1889, d. 31 Aug 1972), m. (1) 1925 Charles H. Edwards (d. 15 Dec 1936); m. (2) 3 Nov 1945 Vernon V. Sparks (b. 21 Sep 1878, d. 6 Jul 1977)

  b. George Albert Woodruff (b. 18 Jun 1890, d. 5 Jun 1923), m. 1 Oct 1913 Beulah Schraier (b. 15 Jun 1896, d. 16 Dec 1960)

  c. Blanche Woodruff (b. 13 May 1892, d. 19 Jun 1966), m. 7 Oct 1920 Earl T. Brown (b. 13 Jun 1890, d. 7 Dec 1940)

  d. Amanda Loverna Woodruff (b. 24 Sep 1893, d. 23 Jul 1978), m. Ivan Nelson (b. 28 Jan 1897, d. 1 Mar 1978)

  e. Hazel Elenore Woodruff (b. 1 Sep 1895, d. 3 Sep 1977), m. 14 Aug 1920 Glen Rohrer (b. 19 Dec 1897, d. 24 Apr 1966)

  f. Zaccheus Woodruff (b. 1 Jan 1898, d. 21 Dec 1900)

APPENDIX B

    g. Rachel Woodruff (b. 22 Jul 1899, d. 31 May 1995), m. (1) 28 May 1927 Viven McDole (b. 14 Mar 1898, d. 15 Jul 1936), m. (2) 20 Nov 1962 Cash C. Crawford (b. 1902)

    h. Seth Rees Woodruff (b. 15 Nov 1901, d. 8 Nov 1947). Unmarried.

    i. Hildred Woodruff (b. 1 Jan 1904, d. 20 May 1952), m. 29 Nov 1934 Floyd Milton Stringham (28 Nov 1902, d. 3 Oct 1966)

    j. Beulah F. Woodruff (b. 12 Feb 1906, d. 24 Oct 1996). Unmarried.

    k. Clarence Abraham Woodruff (b. 27 Mar 1908, d. 11 Mar 1972), m. 22 Dec 1928 Mina Lee Dodd (b. 22 Dec 1910)

    l. Benjamin Franklin Woodruff (b. 21 Dec 1909, d. 13 Jan 1945), m. 19 Nov 1942 Blanche M. Woods

6. *Lewis Woodruff (b. 30 Mar 1868, d. 17 Nov 1929), m. 4 Feb 1889 Alice C. Jennings (b. 20 Nov 1870, d. 18 Feb 1931). Children:*

    a. Albert E. Woodruff (b. 22 Jun 1890, d. 29 Dec 1985), m. Beulah Harvey (b. 27 Nov 1888, d. 23 Aug 1973)

    b. Grace Woodruff (b. 4 Jan 1892, d. 12 Mar 1982), m. 1928 Charles C. Cooper (b. 1875, d. 1947)

    c. Hiram Harold Woodruff (b. 14 Jun 1894, d. 1980), m. 31 Dec 1917 Aura Birch (b. 1898, d. 1958)

    d. Cora May Woodruff (b. 9 May 1896, d. 20 Dec 1986), m. 21 May 1919 Amaziah "Maizie" Don Smith.

    e. Harold Hiram Woodruff (b. 15 Apr 1898, d. 13 Aug 1988), m. Beulah Cyr (b. 6 Mar 1902, d. 10 Jan 1979)

    f. Esther Nellie Woodruff (b. 8 Nov 1899, d. 19 May 1998), m. 4 Aug 1922 Albert Newhall (b. 8 Dec 1898, d. 18 Aug 1964)

    g. Naomi Florence Woodruff (b. 21 Dec 1905, d. 26 May 1983), m. (?) Jordan

    h. Joshua (Josiah) Woodruff (b. 21 Dec 1905, d. 21 Dec 1905)

    i. James William Woodruff (b. 16 Feb 1913, d. 21 Aug 1987), m. 16 Jun 1943 Lulu Viola Carlson (b. 31 Aug 1913, d. 22 Jan 2008)

7. *Margaret Woodruff (b. 6 Feb 1870, d. 8 Feb 1870)*

8. *Anna A. Woodruff (b. 6 Feb 1870, d. 8 Feb 1870)*

9. *Clark Woodruff (b. 18 Sep 1871, d. 22 Feb 1957), m. Sep 1899 Marie (Mamie) Mottin (b. 21 Dec 1876, d. 26 Jan 1946). Children:*

    a. Julius Hiram Woodruff (b. 13 Apr 1900, d. 2 Mar 1995), m. 1 Aug 1923 Olive Mae Fuller (b. 4 Aug 1902, d. 23 Jan 1989)

10. *Jessie Woodruff (b. 16 Mar 1874, d. 9 Aug 1949), m. 15 Nov 1890 Ulysses G. Travis (b. 14 Aug 1869, d. 4 Apr 1969). Children:*

    a. Bessie J. Travis (b. 16 Jan 1893, d. 16 Jan 1981), m. (1) 1912 Daniel F. Smith (b. 13 Aug 1886, d. 13 Aug 1940), m. (2) (?) Beecher.

    b. Ortha Grant Travis (b. 15 Dec 1896, d. 3 Jul 1958), m. (1) 1917 Lucy Jane McCracken (b. 4 Oct 1897, d. 10 Dec 1918) m. (2) 1921 Daisy Wauneta Misner (b. 10 Dec 1902, d. 27 Jan 1994)

    c. Wallace Irving Travis (b. 16 Jan 1904, d. 2 Apr 1986), m. 31 May 1928 Gladys Quakenbush (b. 31 May 1910, d. 14 Mar 2011)

11. *Linnie Woodruff (b. 21 Sep 1876, d. 2 Dec 1899). Unmarried, no children.*

12. *Dora Woodruff (b. 13 Jun 1879, d. 10 Jul 1966), m. 5 Jun 1906 James Franklin Hawkins (b. 21 May 1879, d. 6 Mar 1963) Children:*

    a. Alma May Hawkins (b. 18 Apr 1907, d. 25 Oct 1988), m. Lafayette J. McClain (b. 22 Aug 1906, d. 16 Mar 1989)

    b. Clarence Hawkins (b. 4 Aug 1909, d. 29 May 1991), m. 1929 Doris Mildred Ferguson (b. 24 Jun 1912, d. 1 Jun 2006)

David Woodruff

David Woodruff (b. 22 Nov 1845, d. 8 Oct 1914), m. 1871 Victoria B. Browning (b. 3 Jan 1855, d. 13 Jan 1893). Children:

1. *Carl Woodruff (b. 12 Apr 1873, d. 10 Jan 1886)*
2. *Lulu May (June) Woodruff (b. 11 Aug 1874, d. 31 Jan 1950), m. 19 Apr 1900 Ambrose Booten Fry (b. 23 Jun 1874, d. 31 Jan 1950). Children:*
    a. David Earl Fry (b. 1 Feb 1901, d. 10 Feb 1975), m. 8 Mar 1924 Rosella Wightman (b. 10 Mar 1900, d. 13 Mar 1995)
    b. Vernon Ambrose Fry (b. 7 Oct 1902, d. 16 Oct 1988), m. 14 May 1927 Violet Genevieve Reyman (b. 25 Mar 1902, d. 16 Oct 1991)
    c. Thomas Russell Fry (b. 21 Oct 1907, d. 8 Dec 1982), m. circa 29 Dec 1942 Anna Josephine Johnson (b. 1 Sep 1914, d. 26 Apr 1995)
    d. Harley Milton Fry (b. 5 Apr 1919, d. 8 Jan 1995), m. 10 Sep 1941 Margaret Naomi Parsons (b. 28 Apr 1917, d. 2 Nov 2002)
3. *Arthur C. Woodruff (b. 28 May 1877, d. 14 Sep 1940), m. 25 Feb 1900 Mary Maude McDonald (b. 6 Apr 1874, d. 15 Apr 1947). Children:*
    a. Joseph Duane Woodruff (b. 15 Jan 1905, d. 13 Feb 1956), m. Ina Nadine Neil (b. 6 May 1908, d. 1 May 2003)
    b. Mildred Genevieve Woodruff (b. 15 Sep 1907, d. 16 May 2001), m. Frank A. Willard (b. 15 Apr 1905, d. 10 Jun 2005)
    c. Clive Donald Woodruff (b. 5 Dec 1914, d. 21 Jul 1973), m. Margaret May Mooney (b. 23 Jul 1918, d. 6 Dec 1994)
4. *Edmond Silas Woodruff (b. 15 Sep 1878, d. 11 Apr 1960), m. 7 Jan 1903 Cora May Buell (b. 7 Jan 1879, d. 1961). Children:*
    a. Beulah Luretta Woodruff (b. 19 Feb 1905, d. 26 Mar 1999), m. 3 Jun 1939 Marion L. Swaggart (b. 9 May 1907, d. Jul 1969)
    b. Lillian Victoria Woodruff (b. 5 Aug 1907, d. 2006), m. 10 Jun 1936 Wilber J. Piller (b. 13 Mar 1901, d. 19 Mar 1977)
    c. Edith Pauline Woodruff (b. 31 May 1913, d. 1 Dec 2003), m. 28 Aug 1935 Glenn O. Barleen (b. 4 Apr 1909, d. 4 Oct 1983)

        d.   Carl Edmond Woodruff (b 14 Oct 1915, d. 2000), m. 30 Aug 1941 Mary Alexander (b. 22 May 1918)

5. *Emmette Woodruff (b. 4 Aug 1882, d. circa 1916), m. 27 Nov 1902 Ruby Woodworth (b 1884, d. Nov 1950). Children:*
    a. Leah Anna (Harriet) Woodruff (b. 8 Jul 1903, d. 20 Jun 1921), m. 7 Aug 1920 Ernest George Anderson (b. 1888)
    b. Gladys Victoria Woodruff (b. 3 Nov 1904, d. 18 Feb 1980), m. 1923 Martin James Dermody (b. 1900, d. 1980)
    c. Doris Nola Woodruff (b. 3 Nov 1905, d. 18 Sep 1977), m. 19 Apr 1925 Rev. John Frederick Lippe Sr. (b. 24 Feb 1902, d. 2 Jul 1958)
    d. Allie Imogen Woodruff (b. 1908, d. 18 Jul 1909)

6. *Ethel Leona Woodruff (b. 9 Oct 1884, d. 2 Dec 1967), m. 22 Feb 1903 Ray L. Austin (b. 14 Sep 1880, d. 18 Sep 1963). Children:*
    a. Erma Vera Austin (b. 29 Jun 1904, d. 2 May 1997), m. 1 Jun 1927 Carl August Richard (b. 23 Dec 1900, d. 30 Jun 1977)
    b. Lawrence Woodruff Austin (b. 24 Dec 1906, d. 16 May 1978), m. 3 Aug 1931 Dorothea Arbuthnot (b. 12 Jun 1905, d. 19 Oct 1971)
    c. Harold L. Austin (b. 24 Aug 1911, d. 2 Apr 1998), m. 1933 Cheradel R. Cosley (b. 31 Oct 1911, d. 27 Mar 2004)

7. *Pearl Lena Woodruff (b. 18 Mar 1891, d. 30 Jan 1937), m. 14 Feb 1917 Harrison M. Chesebro (b. 14 Oct 1885, d. 9 May 1954). Children:*
    a. Wayne Harrison Chesebro (b. 13 Jun 1918, d. 16 Feb 2005), m. 7 Apr 1946 Hazel Elvera Nichols (b. 16 Dec 1919, d. 15 Mar 2003)
    b. Ruth Harriet Chesebro (b. 19 May 1922, d. 12 Jan 2010), m. 7 Jan 1943 John Daniel Trude (b. 23 Oct 1918, d. 16 Nov 1991)

Anson Woodruff

Anson Woodruff (b. 23 Apr 1848, d. 15 Mar 1938), m. 17 Apr 1877 Anna Jane Neill (b. 10 Apr 1854, d. 4 Dec 1928). Children:

1. *James Anson Woodruff (b. 5 Feb 1878, d. 31 Dec 1937), m. 18 Feb 1909 Edna Hubbard (b. 1882, d. 25 Jan 1930). Children:*

    a. Gene Neil Woodruff (b. 15 Dec 1910, d. 27 May 1976), m. circa 20 Jun 1940 Harriet Omega Cartwright (b. 1915, d. 13 Apr 1999)

2. *William Woodruff (b. 16 Mar 1879, d. 16 Aug 1948), m. 26 Nov 1913 Carrie Marie Cordell (b. 13 Aug 1895, d. 20 Jun 1969). Children:*

    a. Richard Scott Woodruff (b. 16 Jul 1914, d. 27 Mar 1957). Unmarried.

    b. James Roscoe Woodruff (b. 19 Jul 1915, d. 22 Jan 1989), m. 19 Oct 1940 Gertrude C. Summer (b. 23 Jan 1920, d. 11 Jun 1993)

    c. William Cordell Woodruff (b. 3 Oct 1916, d. 1 Dec 1951), m. (1) 7 Feb 1938 Vivian Audrey Hardow (b. 15 Feb 1919), (2) 29 Dec 1950 Arville Auvon Rinaldi (b. 10 Sep 1922, d. 24 Mar 2004)

    d. Howard Clark Woodruff (b. 16 Apr 1918, d. 16 Oct 1998), m. (1) 28 Sep 1941 Pauline Jane Workman (b. 9 Jul 1925, d. 3 Sep 1971), m. (2) 28 Sep 1973 Janet Helen Coryea (b. 8 Apr 1935)

    e. Lena Alice Woodruff (b. 29 Apr 1920, d. 27 Mar 2011), m. 24 Aug 1937 Benjamin Franklin Long (b. 31 Dec 1915, d. 1 Jun 2002)

    f. Fannie Mildred Woodruff (b. 20 Jan 1923, d. 3 Nov 1964), m. Ervin Austin Dysert (b. 26 Jun 1899, d. 17 Aug 1999)

    g. Sarah Ann Woodruff (b. 12 Sep 1924, d. 8 Jul 2016), m. (1) Ed Lowell, m. (2) John K. Matthews Jr., m. (3) 14 Jul 1973 Wilber Willis Carnes (b. 2 Feb 1915, d. 29 Jan 2002)

    h. David Anson Woodruff (b. 13 Jan 1927, d. 7 Jun 1970), m. 10 May 1951 Earleane Faurot (b. 26 Sep 1929, d. 26 May 1951)

    i. Charles Oscar Woodruff (b. 20 Jul 1928, d. 31 Jan 2004), m. 1947 Joyce Mae Evans (b. 3 Nov 1925, d. 5 Nov 2001)

j. Nancy Joanna Woodruff (b. 30 Aug 1930, d. 8 Feb 2013), m. 27 Feb 1948 Alton Kenneth Woolf (b. 19 Dec 1928, d. 4 Aug 2007)

k. Mariette Woodruff (b. 8 Feb 1932, d. 28 Jun 1998), m. Robert Joseph Wootton (b. 22 Jan 1932, d. 16 Apr 2022)

l. Silas Wayne Woodruff (b. 14 Aug 1934, d. 2 Jan 2013), m. (1) 14 Dec 1952 Florence Irene Brooks (b. 15 May 1927, d. 18 Jun 2004) m. (2) 8 Feb 1964 Ivil Gusty Looney (b. 19 Sep 1931, d. 19 Aug 2015)

3. *Silas Woodruff (b. 12 Feb 1882, d. 29 Apr 1954), m. 14 May 1919 Johanna Neilson (b. 9 May 1887, d. 29 Nov 1960). Children:*

   a. Mary Jane Woodruff (b. 15 Mar 1920, d. 30 Mar 2012), m. Edwin Elias Hamlyn (b. 12 Aug 1910, d. 1 Apr 1986)

4. *Annie May Woodruff (b. 13 Jul 1884, d. 18 Mar 1885)*

5. *Charles Scott Woodruff (b. 3 Jan 1888, d. 15 Mar 1958), m. 22 Nov 1917 Myra Christin (b. 13 Nov 1886, d. Jun 1965). Children:*

   a. Neil Parker Woodruff (b. 25 Jul 1920, d. 10 Oct 2003), m. 15 Jun 1952 Dorothy Adele Russ (b. 25 Nov 1920, d. 23 Jul 2004)

   b. Leslie Scott Woodruff (b. 14 Oct 1922, d. 15 Nov 1953), m. 1946 Lily Alice Anderson (b. 19 Oct 1923, d. 9 Mar 2011)

   c. William Byron Woodruff (b. 12 Sep 1924, d. 5 May 2007). Unmarried.

6. *Bennie Woodruff (b. 17 Apr 1890, d. 10 Sep 1890).*

7. *Lena Joanna Woodruff (b. 19 Dec 1892, d. 4 Dec 1961), m. Leslie Robert Gerhardt (b. 30 May 1892, d. 23 Jul 1938). No children.*

8. *Fannie Mariah Woodruff (b. 19 Feb 1895, d. 12 Jun 1956). Unmarried, no children.*

Appendix C

Early Woodruff Line

England

There are many published volumes devoted to the history of this Woodruff line (such as those about the Woodruffs of New Jersey, of Long Island, and of Fordwich). While some information is shared among all, each book gives additional facts or delves into a topic in more detail. A few texts (such as the records of Southampton and Long Island) are centered only on the events occurring in their locality.

Since their publication, additional information has been unearthed that helps give a more complete understanding of events.

Below, all these sources have been summarized, providing a general picture of this branch of the Woodruff family. All published texts are listed in the Bibliography.

The Cloud County Woodruffs are descendants of the line that originated in the town of Fordwich, Kent, England. "Woodruff" (and its myriad variations) is a fairly common surname.

There are two opinions on its origin. Some published sources claim it is derived from "Wood-reeve,"[70] the governor or keeper of a wood; a forester or bailiff. Other authorities claim it is from the Middle English term "Woderove," or "Woodruff," a sweet-scented plant. In this sense, it would indicate someone who lived where this plant grew in abundance or used it as a perfume.

According to family lore, the line is related to the Woodruffs of Woolley Manor, Wakefield, Yorkshire, England. This relationship is possible—but it is improbable, for several reasons. First, no records have ever been located to confirm it. Moreover, the geography suggests otherwise. Woolley Manor in Wakefield, Yorkshire, is easily 250 miles from Fordwich, Kent—at least 10 days' travel and halfway across the Kingdom of England. In the Middle Ages, this would have been a long and dangerous journey.

Another aspect to consider is social standing. The Yorkshire Woodruffs were a landed family and, in the general class system of the time, were gentry—that is, minor nobility with land and an estate. Sir Richard Woodruff, knight bachelor, was the first of five generations to occupy Woolley Hall.[71] His son, Thomas Woodruffe, succeeded him. While Thomas's death (1549) occurred at nearly the same time as that of Thomas Woodruffe of Fordwich (1552), it seems highly improbable that a landed head of an estate would leave and take up residence in an obscure hamlet in the southern part of the realm. It has been noted that both had sons named William and that both Williams are recorded as having two sons. While this may be an indication of a connection, the question remains why Thomas would abandon his estate and remove himself with only one son, leaving his heir and 10 other children behind.[72]

---

70 During England's Anglo-Saxon period (500 to 1000 AD), a reeve "represented the lord of a district... he levied his lord's dues, and performed some of his judicial functions" (Chamber's Encyclopedia).
71 Joseph Hunter, Rev., *South Yorkshire and the History and Topography of the Deanery of Doncaster*, vol. 2 (1831), p. 387.
72 William Flower, Esq., *Visitation of Yorkshire in the Years 1563 and 1564* (London: Mitchell and Hughes, 1881).

It is possible that the Kent line is only distantly related to the Yorkshire line. It could be that Thomas of Fordwich is the descendant of a younger son or an even more distant relation. Finding records from the Middle Ages to prove lineage can be difficult at the best of times. Tracing a younger child who did not inherit land or title may be impossible.

Lastly, it is likely that these Woodruffs are part of an entirely different line than those in Woolley Hall. Research has turned up Woodruff families in Devonshire, Canterbury, and Dover, among others;[73] Canterbury and Dover are in Kent, and they are a more likely place of origin for that line. Some of these families had standing and means. While the Fordwich Woodruffs were shown to be men of means and some standing, it does not prove they were from the Yorkshire line.

While there are many reasons why the connection is improbable, there are some that suggest it may be possible.

The facts are that both lines had a Thomas Woodruff who lived (and died) at approximately the same time. Both had sons named William, who in turn had two sons. The Yorkshire Woodruffs were a landed gentry family; likewise, Thomas Woodruff was a man of affluence and status from the time he first appeared in Fordwich town and church records

Then there are hints in the royal correspondence. In *Letters and Papers, Foreign and Domestic Henry VIII*, Woodruffs are referenced. A letter regarding the coronation of Henry VIII lists a "Thomas Woodruff" as an usher.[74] A letter two years later states: "Sir Richard Woodrof, of Woolley, York. Exemption from serving on Juries, &c. Greenwich, q5 March, 2Hen. VIII. Del. Canterbury, 28 March."[75]

---

73   Michael Woodruff (1612–1682), who emigrated to the Connecticut colony, was from Cambridge, Cambridgeshire. He was not related to the Fordwich Woodruffs.

74   24 June 1509.

75   29 March 1511.

It has been suggested that because the letter was delivered to Canterbury, Sir Richard of Woolley and his son Thomas might have been residing there and not at their estate in Wakefield. This is possible, but the evidence is not conclusive.

Both Sir Richard and Thomas Woodruff of Woolley left wills that were proved. Searches have not yet turned up these wills; when they are located, perhaps they will provide information that can resolve this question.

Fordwich, England

The Cloud County Woodruffs can definitely be traced back to the late Middle Ages, to the small English town of Fordwich in Kent, England. Nestled on the banks of the river Stour, just a few miles below Canterbury, it is the smallest municipality in England with a town council. It is also one of the oldest settlements, having been mentioned in the Domesday Book of 1066.[76] In earlier days, it was situated on an estuary and was a seaport of some importance. During the twelfth and thirteenth centuries, Norman shipments of stone landed there, to be hauled upriver for the reconstruction of Canterbury Cathedral. Silt deposits slowly removed the town from the sea until it was further upriver.

The town's original name was probably *Fiord-wic*, meaning "bay [*wic*] on the arm of the sea [*fiord*]."[77] This would square with the fact it was a very old town and was once a seaport.

The following is the Fordwich-Woodruff line that can be documented:[78]

---

76 Completed in 1086 for William the Conqueror, it was a comprehensive survey of much of England and Wales, with detailed information about the land, people, and resources at the time.

77 C. E. Woodruff, *History of the Town and Port of Fordwich* (Canterbury, Kent, UK: Cross & Jackman, 1895), p. 2.

78 The lettering (A–D) is used backwards for the same reason as "A.D." and "B.C." dates, which count away from the birth of Christ. In this case, the demarcation point is the first generation emigrating to America. English generations are lettered, while American ones are numbered.

D. Thomas Woodrove, 1508–1552

C. William Woodroffe, d. 1587

B. Robert Woodroffe, d. 1611

A. John Woodroffe, 1574–1611

They were definitely freemen;[79] some early church and town records also refer to them as "yeoman."[80] All held significant positions of authority, performing various public and/or parish duties.

The earliest known record of this Woodruff line appears in 1508, with a note of payment by Thomas Woodrove to the churchwardens for the rent of his house.

Thomas performed duties that normally belonged to the town's clerk, so although he may not have been specifically designated as such, he was very likely acting in that capacity. The abbot of St. Augustine's Abbey just outside Canterbury was lord and mayor of Fordwich. When the mayor held court, it was a requirement that the abbot's bailiff be present. In 1509 and 1510, Thomas rode to the Isle of Thanet[81] to fetch him. A few years later, he rode to Westminster to pay a fine incurred by a fellow townsman. He eventually became a town jurat,[82] a high position of authority. According to the *History of the Town of Fordwich*:

> *The Mayor and Jurats were Justices of the Peace within the liberty [town], by virtue of their office, and possessed a practically unlimited jurisdiction in criminal, as well as civil, cases. To the Mayor and Jurats belonged the right of administering the goods of intestates, of granting probate of wills, and acting as coroner in all cases within the liberty.*[83]

---

79 Someone not a serf or slave, with privileges of the borough or city.
80 An official providing an honorable service in a royal or noble household, ranking between a squire and a page.
81 A peninsula in the easternmost part of Kent. At one time, it was an actual island, separated from the mainland by a wide channel.
82 In Fordwich, a jurat was apparently both a magistrate and municipal councilor combined in a single office—a position of some authority.
83 C. E. Woodruff, *History of the Town and Port of Fordwich* (Canterbury, Kent, UK: Cross & Jackman, 1895), pp. 56–57.

He was a person of some means and became a considerable property holder. Documents from the Fordwich monuments chest,[84] 9th, Henry VIII, report that in 1538, Thomas owned "2 messuages,[85] 3 gardens, 30 acres of arable land, 5 acres of meadow, and 8 acres of meadow" in Fordwich.

Also in 1538, as part of Henry VIII's suppression of the monasteries, Thomas sat with other jurats to decide on the disposition of the assets and property of St. Augustine's Abbey for the crown. Thomas Woodrove died in approximately 1552.

Son William Woodroffe was next to appear in the town records. First mentioned in 1550 in the era of Queen Elizabeth I, he became a jurat in 1579, possibly a senior jurat, as he signed the minutes of the court. He was also keeper of the town chest, which was used for safeguarding deeds, other important records or documents, and fees. This was a position of immense trust and responsibility. William died in 1587, leaving two sons, Robert and William Jr.

William Sr. and both his sons appear in the town muster roll of 1573.[86] It states that "Willyam Wodruf thelder wt his men Robert Woodruffe… [issued] one calyver[87] furnished one almon rivett[88] furnished." Further down the muster list, it is recorded that "William Woodruf the younger [furnished] sword and dager."

Robert died in 1611, but William Jr. lived until at least 1614; the town muster roll indicates that he was furnished a musket that year.

It was during William Sr.'s time that the current Fordwich town hall was erected. Originally the ground floor was a prison for petty criminals; the first floor served as a courtroom. Acting as the meeting place for the town council, it has served Fordwich continuously for

---

84 A chest used to store records of the Fordwich town council. This chest, containing the earliest town records, dates back to the fifteenth century.
85 A piece of land used, or intended to be used, as a site for a dwelling.
86 A list of able-bodied men able to serve in the town militia, if required.
87 A handgun discharged from the shoulder.
88 Light flexible armor.

nearly 500 years. It is listed in the United Kingdom as a Grade II building.[89]

Robert Woodruff (1544–1611) and brother William were both listed in the town books as freemen. Robert was on record as being both a town jurat and, in 1584, a churchwarden.[90] In 1572, he married Alice Russell of St. Mary's Northgate. From this union they had two children: John (b. 1574) and William.

One note of interest is that Shakespeare may have performed in Fordwich. On 6 October 1605, the town paid the King's Players[91] 10 shillings to put on a show in Fordwich. The show would have been attended primarily by men of means and status in the community. With his standing as senior jurat, Robert would have most certainly attended. So Robert Woodroffe (and possibly his son John) very likely attended a play that was not only written by Shakespeare but also featured him on stage.

Robert died during the reign of James I, around 1611.

Robert's eldest son, John, took up residence in Northgate, where his uncle, William Russell, was churchwarden. In 1601 he married Elizabeth Cartwright; they had one son, whom they also named John and who was baptized in 1604.[92]

Robert's son John, like his father, died around 1611. John died at the age of 36, leaving a widow and seven-year-old son. Even in that era, it was unusual for a person of means to die at such a young age, let alone die around the same time as their father. Although the Black Plague officially ended in the fourteenth century, periodic outbreaks of this deadly disease (the bubonic plague) still arose. One such epidemic occurred around this time. So it is likely that both Robert and his son John fell victim to it.

---

89 Buildings that are of special interest.
90 Lay official in a parish of the church.
91 Leading London-based theater company of which Shakespeare was a member and for which he wrote his plays.
92 Seven consecutive generations named their sons John. One named two of their sons John. This and the inaccuracy or lack of early records has caused considerable confusion in tracing this family.

In such dark and turbulent times, it was not safe for a woman to live alone without protection. In 1611—shortly after her husband John's death—Elizabeth Cartwright married John Gosmer, churchwarden and witness to her late husband's will. According to *Canterbury Marriage Licenses, 1568-1618*, a marriage license was issued 24 October 1611 in Mary Bredin Parish, Canterbury, to "Gosmer, John of St. Mary Northgate, Canterbury, Joiner, and Elizabeth Woodruffe of same parish, widow."

John Gosmer

John Woodruff, along with his mother, Elizabeth, and stepfather, John Gosmer, returned to St. Mary's Northgate. At the age of 32, young John Woodruff served as churchwarden. A year later, he married Ann, whose surname is unknown. Their first child, John, was baptized in 1637 in the parish of Sturry, half a mile from Fordwich.

Not much is known about John Gosmer's life before he married Elizabeth Cartwright. Available records indicate he was the first of his line in the town of Fordwich; the earliest mention of him is in 1611, where he was witness to John Woodruff's will. In 1613, John Gosmer, sidesman (churchwarden's assistant), signed a bill of "Christenings, Marriages, and Burials in the Parish of St. Mary, Northgate."

Little is known of his family. Prior to marrying Elizabeth (Cartwright) Woodruff, he had been married and had at least one child. *The Woodruff Chronicles* (vol. 1, page 35) states there is a record of a deceased brother who had children, a daughter named Elizabeth (who later lived with her uncle), and probably a son named John. In *Canterbury Marriage Licenses, 1619-1660*, an entry on page 612 reads:

> *Thomas Lee of Saint Peter's parish, Canterbury, fellmonger, bachelor, aged about 23 years, with his father's consent testified*

by John Cartwright, cordwainer, and Elizabeth Gosmer of Fordwich, virgin, aged about 23 years, now under the government of her uncle, John Gosmer of same parish, who hath brought her up and now consents.

The Canterbury marriage license records also show that a John Gosmer, a bachelor and joiner of Saint Mary Northgate, married Ann Woodruff, a widow.[93] She was later widowed again and remarried Richard Carter; the two relocated to Massachusetts colony.[94]

John Gosmer rose to a position of prominence in the community. He was listed in the town muster roll of 1637 as "John Gosmer, gent."[95] That same year, there was a dispute between him and the Fordwich Corporation[96] regarding the extent of rights over a particular parcel of land. Apparently, this was successfully resolved, as one year later, Gosmer was mayor of Fordwich.

---

93 Her first husband's name is unknown; conjecture is that he was a descendant of the original Thomas Woodrove in Fordwich.

94 John Gosmer purchased property in Boston, which he gave in 1658 to "kinswoman Ann, widow of Richard Carter."

95 A gentleman at the time was a man who was entitled to bear arms but who was not part of the nobility.

96 A "corporation" was the medieval form of town government, usually consisting of aldermen ("elders") or others of high status. Usually a mayor was elected.

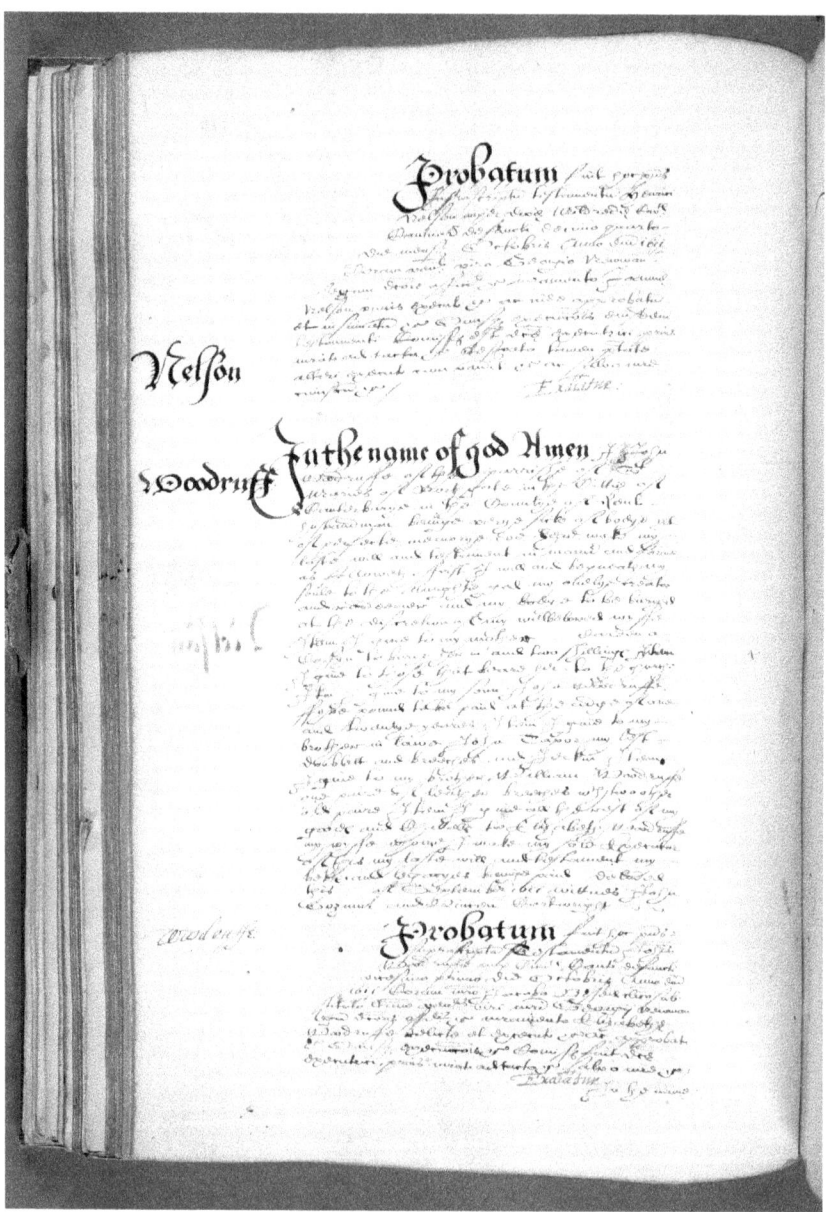

Copy of John(A) Woodroffe's will, dated 1611. Witnessed by John Gosmer.

APPENDIX C

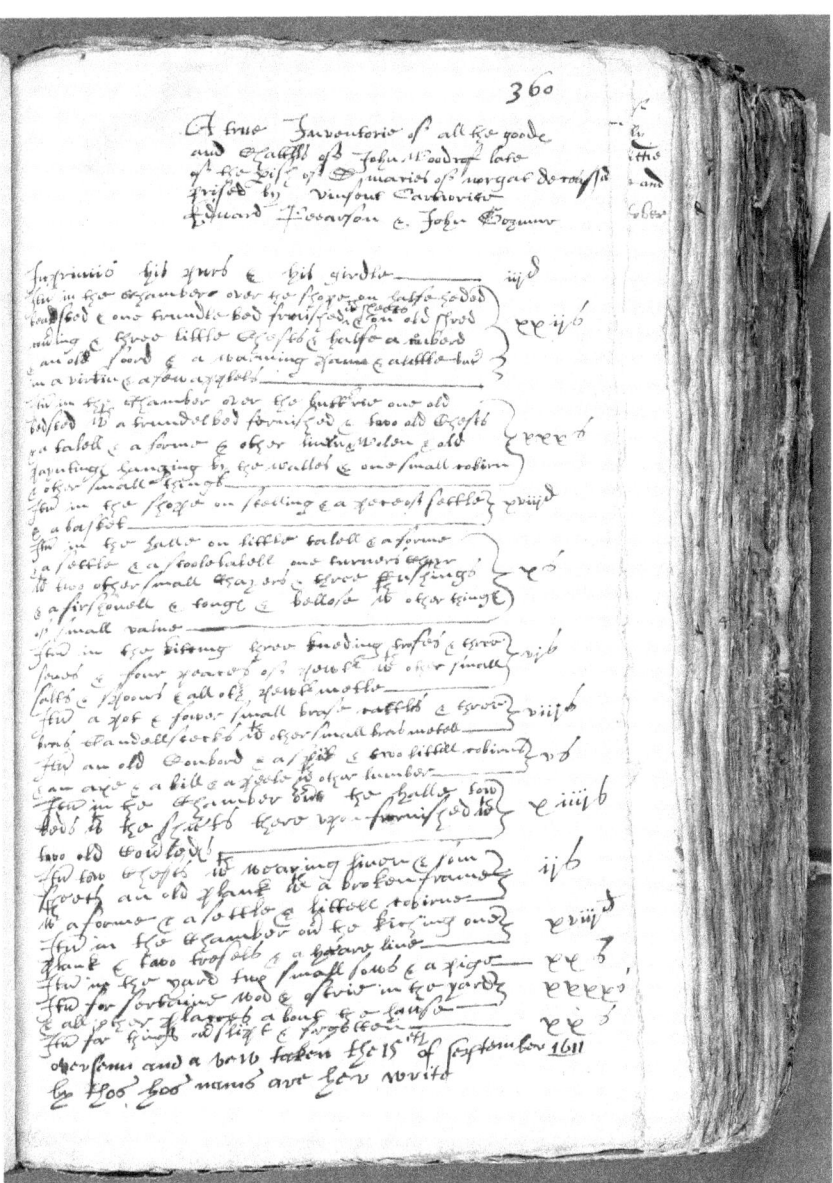

Inventory of John(A) Woodroffe's estate, 1611.

Emigration to America

It was the reign of King Charles I. Political and religious tensions were rising and would soon come to a boil. The English Civil War was on the horizon.

Charles I, facing major financial difficulties, was frustrated by Parliament's refusal to approve money for a budget or to fund wars he wanted to wage.

There were few taxes that English monarchs could impose without approval from Parliament. One in particular, the "ship tax," was originally imposed on port towns during times of war. Its purpose was to pay for ships of the Royal Navy and thus repel both pirates and sovereign enemies. However, Charles enacted the tax in peacetime and levied it not only on coastal areas but also on inland communities.

Many of the towns resisted paying this tax, including the ports, Fordwich among them. Many disputed the validity of the tax; quite a few (including London) claimed exemption, and some municipalities refused to pay.[97] Charles arranged for a series of sitting judges to rule that the ship tax was legal. Three writs were levied by the king under this guise in three successive years, starting in 1634.

Gosmer was mayor of the Corporation in 1638. He disappeared from Fordwich history after this year; there is no further mention of him. In 1639, the Council in Whitehall demanded from the mayor of Fordwich an unpaid tax assessment from 1638, "which should long since have been paid to the Sheriff or Kent or the treasurer of the Navy." Gosmer had been a prominent public figure the previous year. Other records show that by then, he had left England and immigrated to the American colonies.

Examinations through the years have not found any record of his departure. It should be noted, however, that only passengers who

---

97 Imposition of the ship tax was one of the causes of the English Civil War.

departed legally appeared on ships' passenger lists.[98] As he probably departed (like many others did) to avoid payment of the ship tax—and possible imprisonment—it is understandable that there would not be a record of his passage.

Traveling with him were his wife, Elizabeth Cartwright; his stepson John;[99] and John's wife and their infant son, John (called "the Elder"), who was baptized in 1637. This was a difficult and dangerous journey to embark on with a one-year-old child; they must have had a compelling reason to travel quickly.[100]

Records show that some of John Gosmer's relations (son Richard, kinswoman Ann, and her husband Richard Carter) were also early arrivals in Massachusetts. It is possible that all made the journey together.

Regardless of the circumstances under which they traveled, it has been established that John Gosmer and family were in the colonies by 1639. Thus, they became the first Woodruffs to arrive in America.[101]

---

98 Records have shown other passengers with the name of Woodruff. Those found to date have been found to be unrelated and part of other Woodruff lines.

99 This stepson is referred to as John "the Immigrant" Woodruff and is considered the first generation in American genealogical reckoning: "John(1)."

100 Another strong reason favoring the argument that the family secretly fled to avoid the consequences of the ship tax.

101 This predates Matthew Woodruff—no relation—who emigrated from Hartford to Connecticut in 1640–1641.

1888. Cora Woodruff with husband Thomas McClure and son Irving.

Appendix D

Southampton Woodruffs

On 10 March 1639, a charter was issued in Lynn, Massachusetts, to establish a new colony. There were eight settler families (referred to as "undertakers") in the original proposal.

The undertakers purchased a sloop for £80. Prior to sailing, the group disposed of their interest in the vessel to Captain Daniel Howe. He would take ownership of the boat; in exchange, he would deliver them to their new charter location and return three times annually for the next two years to transport goods from the Lynn colony to their new home. A document disposing of the vessel was drawn up on 10 May 1639.

According to agreements, the party was authorized to occupy an eight square-mile section anywhere on Long Island. Shortly after the original agreement was made—on 4 June 1640—John Gosmer and family were admitted as undertakers in the enterprise. His family included Wife Elizabeth, stepson John(1)[102] "the Immigrant" Woodruff, his wife Ann, and their young son John(2) "the Elder."

The journey began in May 1649. It was probably short; it was definitely not without adventure. The party arrived at the head of

---

[102] The number in parentheses indicates the generation, so there is no confusion over which John Woodruff is being referenced. Over the first three generations, there were at least nine persons named John, often living in the same town, frequently in the same household.

Cow Bay, Manhasset (Long Island Sound). Once ashore, they found the arms of the Prince of Orange affixed to a tree. This should not have been wholly unexpected, as the Dutch had been in the New World since 1614, nearly as long as the English.

The leader of the company, Lieutenant Howe, pulled down the sign. Later, the nearby Dutch received a report that some "foreign strollers" had come, creating mischief. When Dutch officials arrived, they found the undertakers had already built one house and started building a second. It was reported that the prince's coat of arms had been removed and replaced with "an unhandsome face." After nine days of investigation and questioning, the colonists were not arrested but discharged by the Dutch. They were allowed to leave on 19 May on the condition that they never return without the Dutch officials' express permission. Immediately afterwards, they sailed to the east end of Long Island.

The new land was settled in June. The indigenous people already on the land proved friendly, and the land was "honorably purchased" by the undertakers.

As he had done in Fordwich, John Gosmer took a leading role in the new town. In 1644, he was a town magistrate. Three years later, when Southampton became part of Connecticut, he was one of the first to represent his town in the House of Magistrates in Hartford's General Court, which he did from 1647 to 1650, then again from 1655 to 1658. In 1642 he was the primus[103] of the three Southampton magistrates and so was elected in succession for several years.

Standard practice of the time listed only heads of households, so for many years the name Woodruff did not appear on the rolls (being part of the Gosmer household). In 1657, John(1) appeared on the list of representatives of the town houses; in 1659, he was listed as succeeding his father in the Gosmer homestead.

---

103 A Latin phrase meaning "first among equals." Used to describe a person who has a position of authority or leadership but is still considered equal to other members of the group.

Farming was one of the main industries in the early settlement; whaling was the other. John Gosmer was part of the whaling squadron. In 1657, John(1) succeeded him.

Tragedy struck John Gosmer during this time as well. His only son Richard (who apparently also emigrated) died; his estate was administered in 1650. Gosmer appears to have adopted John(2) "the Elder" as his heir. At about the same time, John(2) "the Younger" was born.[104] John Gosmer died in 1661.

* * *

From the time they first arrived, the undertakers who had become the townsfolk of Southampton had flourished. For two decades, the settlers had worked hard and had a good life to show for their efforts. John(1), while not as publicly visible as his stepfather, was still a valuable member of the community, doing his duty in the whaling squadron and having been elected impounder.[105]

Shifting political winds brought a change of fortune; times suddenly became very hard for Woodruff and his townsmen. On 12 March 1664, Charles II granted Long Island and other territories to his brother James, the Duke of York. In one motion, Southampton was no longer bound to Connecticut and was now part of the Province of New York.

The previous governor in New York was replaced by Francis Lovelace, who apparently ruled with a stern (and arguably brutal) hand. He reportedly remarked that "the only way to keep the people quiet was to lay such taxes upon them as should leave no time for thinking of anything else than how to pay them."[106]

These new circumstances created hardship for all concerned.

---

104 This would explain why John(1) named both of his sons John; it was expected that after adoption, John(2) "the Elder" would assume the Gosmer surname.

105 An official whose duty is to collect and confine stray animals in the community, such as livestock, geese, and swine.

106 F. E. Woodruff, *A Branch of the Woodruff Stock* (Morristown, NJ: The Jerseyman, 1902), p. 23.

This additional stress late in life may have hastened the demise of John(1), who, already "weak in Body," made his will 4 May 1670 and died 1 June 1670, aged 66 years.

John(1) was a wealthy man for his time, judging by the size of other estates and wills from the same period. His estate was divided between his widow, Ann, and his two sons named John. John(2) "the Elder" was given a small token amount. Normally, this would indicate that his share of inheritance had already been received, but it could also mean that he had received his inheritance from his adopted father, John Gosmer. (Records of property sales at the time seem to confirm this.)

He was unquestionably a selfless man with a strong and generous character. In *The Woodruffs of New Jersey*, F. E. Woodruff commented:

> *...a study of the too scanty information within reach has given the impression that had he less selfishly sacrificed himself to the interests of his parents, his family, and his town, the man who was Churchwarden at 32 would have taken up more room in the records. The little there is, however, is to his honor... it may be inferred that he was upright, of tact and sound judgement, and generally, of a character and standing that commanded the confidence and respect of all, both high and low, in the community.*[107]

The family's legacy was in the hands of the two brothers named John. Soon the family would migrate from Southampton and re-establish itself in the history of another colony.

---

107 F. E. Woodruff, *The Woodruffs of New Jersey* (New York: Grafton Press, 1909)

Appendix E

Elizabeth, New Jersey, Woodruffs

With the death of John(1) "the Immigrant" in 1670, the family was now in the hands of the two brothers: John(2) "the Elder" and John(2) "the Younger."

According to the *Woodruff Chronicles* (vol. 2, preface, page x), there are four distinct branches that stem from John(1) "the Immigrant" in Southampton, Long Island:

1. **Long Island Branch**. These are the family members who remained in the Southampton, Long Island, area. Included in this line are those who migrated to Sharon, Connecticut, and vicinity.

2. **Elizabethtown Branch**. This is John(2) "the Elder," wife Sarah Ogden, and their descendants, who migrated from Southampton, Long Island, to Elizabethtown, New Jersey, in 1665.

3. **Cranford-Westfield Branch**. This describes the line of Joseph(3), son of John(2) "the Younger," Joseph's wife

Hannah Ward and their descendants.[108] *It is this line that eventually leads to the Cloud County Woodruffs.*

4. **West Jersey Branch**. This pertains to later migrations of John(2) "the Younger's" family, mostly grandchildren, to Cumberland, West Jersey (now part of New Jersey).

Information on the (2) Elizabethtown Branch and the (3) Cranford-Westfield Branch is briefly included here. The other two lines, the Long Island and West Jersey branches, while valuable, are of no interest to the account of the Cloud County families.

Elizabethtown Branch: John(2) "The Elder" Woodruff

This was the infant son who made the perilous Atlantic voyage with his parents, John(1) and Anne Woodruff.

John(2) "the Elder" married Sarah Ogden[109] around 1659 or 1660. He was already a landowner as early as 1659 or 1660, having received lands from his adopted father, John Gosmer. Their fortunes increased as his father-in-law gave them land, then later another house and home lot.

Their eldest daughter Sarah was born 1660–1661; she died in childhood around 1665. It is possible that the grief of this event caused the elder John(2) to move with his father-in-law to from Southampton, Long Island, to Elizabethtown, New Jersey. There they would have the support of family who were also settling in the area; there was also the promise of more land. So that same year, John "the Elder" sold some of his Southampton homes and holdings

---

108 In early genealogical histories, the Cranford-Westfield Woodruffs were often confused with the Elizabeth Town branch. This is due to information being incomplete and missing at that time. The families lived relatively close to each other, and several given names were used by both. There was likely some intermarriage, and many from each line are buried in the same cemeteries. Both sons John(2) had sons named John and Joseph. This is fully explained and corrected in C. Woodruff and M. R. Herod, *Woodruff Chronicles, a Genealogy*, vol. 2 (Glendale: Arthur H. Clark Company, 1971).

109 Daughter of John Ogden, one of the original undertakers in the colony and a prominent and influential figure.

to his sister Anne and the rest to other townsfolk and relocated to Elizabethtown, New Jersey.

John(2) "the Elder" distinguished himself as a leading citizen in the community. In the Anglo-Dutch War of 1672–1674, he was commissioned as an ensign; in civilian life, he served as high sheriff and as magistrate.

After his wife Sarah's death sometime after 1675, he married Mary Parkhurst. John(2) "the Elder" had 10 children: Sara (1660–1665), John (1665–1722), Jonathan (d. 1691), Joseph Sr. (1675–1746), David (d. before 1732), Daniel (1678–1741), Benjamin (d. 1726), Elizabeth, Sarah, and Hannah.

John(2) "the Elder" died 17 April 1692, in Elizabethtown, New Jersey. In his will, he bequeathed substantial land holdings, money, and possessions to his wife Mary and all of his children.

Cranford-Westfield Branch: John(2) "the Younger" Woodruff

John(2) "the Younger" was born in Southampton; the exact date is unknown, but it was approximately 1650. John Gosmer's son Richard died that year, and Gosmer had adopted John(1)'s older son as his heir. It is plausible to presume the younger son was born after these events; otherwise, it would not make sense to have also named him "John."

When his father John(1) died in 1670, the younger brother John(2) inherited his Southampton estate. He married Hannah Newton c. 1670.[110] Together they raised a family of 10 children: Joseph (1676–1741), Abigail, John (d. before 1703), Samuel (d. 1716), Benjamin (d. 1750), Elizabeth, Nathaniel Sr. (1680–1725), Sarah, Hannah, and Isaac.

---

110 F. E. Woodruff, *The Woodruffs of New Jersey* (New York: Grafton Press, 1909).

It is presumed that the younger John(2) was a good and productive member of the town, but there is nothing recorded to show that he played a notable part in the public arena. The governor at the time, Lovelace, levied excessive taxes on the population. Even though John(2) owned considerable land, it could be expected that with such a large family, he was what was called "land-poor": rich in land but not in money.

He died in 1703. His land and possessions were bequeathed to his wife, Hannah, and his children, all of whom were still living.

Joseph(3) Woodruff

Of John(2) Woodruff "the Younger's" sons, the one of interest is Joseph(3) Woodruff, born in 1676. He grew up in the family's Southampton home but, at the age of 23, decided to relocate to New Jersey, as his older brother had done some years before. He left Southampton, Long Island, in 1697, two years before his father's death.

There were several likely reasons for this decision. His father, despite substantial land holdings, was still land-poor due to excessive taxes collected by the Duke of York. There was also the issue of John(2) the Younger having to provide for such a large family. So Joseph(3) migrated to the colony of New Jersey, where he had influential relatives and there was an abundance of land being distributed. A cousin from Southampton, Robert Woolley, was also migrating there to become an associate[111] of Elizabethtown and acquire a lot in Westfield.

Joseph(3) acquired Lot No. 149, a 100-acre "homestead plantation," in 1701. Over the following years, he toiled and created an admirable home for himself and his family.

---

111 The founders of Elizabeth did not incorporate a town; they formed an association. The inhabitants were "associates." When a boy came of age (at 21 years), he was given his one hundred acres of land.

There is no record of him being active in public affairs in the way that many of his relatives were. But the frontier land he lived in at that time was filled with perils. Forested acres needed to be cleared and transformed into farmland. There were wolves and Indians to defend against. There were armed conflicts with the French. Thus, it is understandable that he did not participate much in civic affairs.

He married his wife, Hannah Ward, in 1700. Together they had 13 children: John(4) "Deacon" (1704–1768), Jonathan(4) Sr. (1707–1777), William(4) (b. 1708), Samuel(4) (1710–1754), Abigail(4) (1712–1766), Joseph(4) Jr., Isaac(4) (1715–1760), Nathaniel(4) (1719–1795), Joanna(4) (b. 1722), Sarah(4) (1722–1793), Thomas(4) (1722–1801), Hezekiah(4) (1724–1776), and Benjamin(4) (1726–1786).

He made his will on 15 January 1742 and died on 2 February the same year. According to his will, he was a prosperous man; he provided money, goods, and/or property to his wife and each of his 13 children, all of whom were still living. He was buried in Lot No. 290 of the cemetery just across from the Westfield First Presbyterian Church. His wife, Hannah, passed away only a few months after him.

John(4) "Deacon" Woodruff

Little is known of Joseph(3)'s eldest son, John(4) Woodruff; according to his tombstone, he was a deacon. Born in 1704, he married Eleanor Donnington around 1750. There were three children from this union: John(5) (1723–1778), Moses(5) "Manassas" Sr. (1734–1817), and Cornelius(5) Sr. (1740–1814), all of whom were named in his will. He died on 24 September 1768 and was buried in Westfield Cemetery, Lot No. 265.

Even less information is available for John(4)'s eldest son, John(5). He was born in 1723. He married Sarah Miller, and together they raised nine children: Eleanor(6) (1749–1796), Abner(6) (1765–

1835), Abigail(6), Rhoda(6) "Caty," Phebe(6), Samuel(6) (d. 1790), Sarah(6), Simeon(6), and Stephen(6) Sr. (d. 1768). John(5) died in 1778.

Appendix F

Washington County, Ohio, Woodruffs

Abner(6) Woodruff was born, according to *Woodruff Chronicles*, volume 2, in Springfield, New Jersey. Along with his brother Samuel(6), he inherited his father's plantation in 1778, when he was only 18 years old. He was a blacksmith by trade. In 1876, he married Catherine Roll, daughter of Isaac Roll[112] and Sarah Cauldwell.

After some time, they moved from Springfield to Redstone, Pennsylvania. A steady stream of settlers was moving westward at that time; around 1798, Abner(6) and Catherine joined this migration, traveling with five children along the Ohio River. Eventually they settled along Wolf Creek in Barlow Township, Washington County, Ohio. This was a heavily wooded area, with rich farmland and abundant game. This is where they established their 100-acre homestead. They were the first Woodruffs in Washington County and one of the early pioneering families to settle in the region.

According to Edmond Silas Woodruff (son of Cloud County's David Woodruff):

> *The first settlers in this community of Barlow, Watertown, Cutler and other small villages, had a difficult time in obtaining*

---

112 Isaac Roll's father, John Roll, was a sergeant in the Revolutionary War.

any money, and money they had to have for some purposes, such as medicine, taxes and other necessities of that nature.

…Up until 1850, nearly all wool, wheat, pork and other farm products were hauled to Marietta, or to Waterford, nine miles distance. The wheat [sold for] 37 ½ [cents] per bushel. They raised but little, but it was necessary to sell it to obtain some money. Eggs brought two to four cents a dozen, which was considered by the farmers as a new road to fortune.[113]-

There has been some disagreement on the number of children born to Abner(6) and Catherine. The *History of Marietta and Washington Counties* lists six. *Woodruff Chronicles*, volume 2, corrects this to seven. However, a comparison of the unpublished manuscript by Abba Lincoln Shepard and a handwritten page from one of Abner Woodruff's granddaughters suggests that there were nine children. These were Polly(7) (1785–1828), Isaac(7) (1787–1861), Nancy(7) (1790–1809), Elias(7) (1793–1877), Hannah(7) (1795–1807), Sarah(7) (b. 1798), Elizabeth(7) "Betsy" (1800–1834), Abner(7) Jr. (1801–1882), and Maria(7) (1806–1807). Their firstborn son, Isaac(7), was named after Catherine's father.

Abner(6) died in Washington County, Ohio, in 1836. His wife followed him two years later.

Isaac(7) Woodruff

Like his father, Isaac(7) was a farmer in Washington County. And like many in the Woodruff line, he held public office, serving as justice of the peace in Barlow Township.

In 1811, he married Margaret Green.[114] Together, they had 10 children: Silas(8) (1813–1905), Maria(8) (1813–1878), Nancy(8)

---

113 A. L. Sheppard, "Woodruff Family History." Unpublished manuscript (n.d.).
114 Daughter of Duty Green, a soldier in the Revolutionary War.

(1815–1871), Jeanette(8) (1817–1901), Parmelia(8) (1819–1914), Caroline(8) (1821–1906), Chester(8) (1823–1881), Duty(8) (1825–1902), John(8) (b. 1830), and Calvin(8) (1832–1861).

Isaac(7)'s wife died in 1853. He died in 1861, aged 73 years.

Silas(8) Woodruff

Born in 1813, Silas(8) lived his entire life on the family homestead established by his father, Silas(7). He extended the original 100-acre farm to 1,780 acres by 1873.[115] The farm was productive, and the surrounding land teemed with wildlife; game was so plentiful that he once shot two deer with a single shot. Another time, 20 men in Barlow Township engaged in a squirrel hunt, shooting 4,216 in all.[116]

He became wealthy when oil was discovered on his property. He built a large home valued at $6,000—a tremendous sum at that time.

He was also well liked and regarded. The *History of Marietta and Washington County, Ohio* describes him thus:

Silas Woodruff is a highly esteemed man, and is noted far and wide for his charity and benevolence.

He was married twice. He married his first wife, Mary Stump, in 1833. Together they had nine children: Isaac(9) (1832), Hiram(9) (1834), Hermann(9) (1835), Sarah(9) (1837), Maria(9) (1842), David(9) (1845), Anson(9) (1848), Mary(9) (1851), and Silas(9) Jr. (1854).

Mary Stump died 7 August 1859. Four months later, Silas(8) married the widow Elizabeth (Young) Stollar. The couple had four more children: Alpharetta(9) (1861–1891), Calvin(9) (1862–1937), Marion(9) (1865–1945), and Clarence(9) (1869–1963).

---

[115] It is possible that the additional acres were Hiram(9)'s old farmland.
[116] M. R. Andrews, *History of Marietta and Washington County, Ohio* (Chicago: Biographical Publishing Company, 1902), p. 226.

Like all families during this time, the Woodruffs were affected by the Civil War. Eight Woodruffs from Washington County served in the Union Army. Four of Silas(8)'s sons were on the list: Anson(9), David(9), Hiram(9), and Isaac(9).[117]

In the last years of his life, Silas(8) was described as being physically feeble and suffering from rheumatism.

Silas(8) died 8 February 1905, aged 93 years, the oldest man in Barlow Township. He was survived by 10 children, 46 grandchildren, and 39 great-grandchildren.

---

117 Anson(9), David(9), and Hiram(9) were the three brothers who settled in Cloud County in 1871.

Photographic Credits

1. Front cover & spine: Pam Coon, Poway, California. Used with permission.
2. Back cover: © 2024, David Hayes, www.photoguppy.com. Author photo.

Pages i-xvii

1. Page i: Pam Coon, Poway, California. Used with permission.
2. Pages ii-iii: Kansas State Historical Society. Used with Permission.
3. Pages v: Kansas State Historical Society. Used with Permission.
4. Pages vi-vii: Kansas State Historical Society. Used with Permission.
5. Page xii: Pam Coon, Poway, California. Used with permission.
6. Page xviii: © 2024, David Hayes, www.photoguppy.com. Author photo.

Chapter 1

1. Page 4: © 2024, David Hayes, www.photoguppy.com. Author photo
2. Page 9: David Hayes, Bangkok, Thailand. Used with permission.

Chapter 2

1. Page 10: Charles Phelps Cushing. Alamy.com Public Domain.
2. Page 14: Pam Coon, Poway, California. Used with permission.

Chapter 3

1. Page 20: Kansas State Historical Society. Used with Permission.
2. Page 25: *Concordia Empire*, Concordia, Kansas, 12 November 1878.
3. Page 29: © 2024, David Hayes, www.photoguppy.com. Author photo.
4. Page 30: Cloud County Clerk and Recorder, Concordia, Kansas. Used with permission.
5. Page 31: Cloud County Clerk and Recorder, Concordia, Kansas., Used with permission.
6. Page 35: Pam Coon, Poway, California. Used with permission.

Chapter 4

1. Page 36: Kansas State Historical Society. Used with permission..
2. Page 39: Pam Coon, Poway, California. Used with permission.
3. Page 41: Pam Coon, Poway, California. Used with permission.
4. Page 42: Pam Coon, Poway, California. Used with permission.

Chapter 5

1. Page 48: Public domain.
2. Page 50: © 2024, David Hayes, www.photoguppy.com. Author photo.
3. Page 52: Pam Coon, Poway, California. Used with permission.
4. Page 54: Pam Coon, Poway, California. Used with permission.
5. Page 56: Pam Coon, Poway, California. Used with permission.
6. Page 57: Pam Coon, Poway, California. Used with permission.

Chapter 6

1. Page 62: Public domain.
2. Page 65: Pam Coon, Poway, California. Used with permission.
3. Page 67: *Concordia Empire*, Concordia, Kansas, 5 February 1903.
4. Page 69 (Top): Pam Coon, Poway, California. Used with permission.

PHOTOGRAPHIC CREDITS

5. Page 69 (Lower): © 2024, David Hayes, www.photoguppy.com. Author photo.
6. Page 71: Paul Huscher, Waukee, Iowa. Used with permission.
7. Page 73: Pam Coon, Poway, California. Used with permission.
8. Page 75: © 2024, David Hayes, www.photoguppy.com. Author photo.
9. Page 76: *Miltonvale Record*, Miltonvale, Kansas, 10 November 1905.
10. Page 80: *Miltonvale Record*, Miltonvale, Kansas, 22 November 1907.
11. Page 81: Cloud County Historical Society, Concordia, Kansas. Used with permission.
12. Page 85: Kansas State Historical Society. Used with Permission.

Chapter 7:

1. Page 92: Public domain.
2. Page 95: Mary Margaret Carroll Richard and Clayton Walker, Parker, Colorado. Used with permission.
3. Page 98: *Concordia Blade-Empire*, Concordia, Kansas, 25 March 1915.
4. Page 99: *Clyde Voice-Republican*, Clyde, Kansas, 22 June 1911.
5. Page 101: *Clyde Republican*, Clyde, Kansas, 22 May 1911.
6. Page 104: Pam Coon, Poway, California. Used with permission.
7. Page 105: David Hayes, Bangkok, Thailand. Used with permission.
8. Page 106: Pam Coon, Poway, California. Used with permission.
9. Page 107: © 2024, David Hayes, www.photoguppy.com. Author photo.
10. Page 109 (Top): *Concordia Daily Kansan*, Concordia, Kansas, 18 December 1912.
11. Page 109 (Lower): *Concordia Daily Kansan*, Concordia, Kansas, 5 June 1915.
12. Page 110: *Concordia Blade-Empire*, Concordia, Kansas, 10 August 1914.
13. Page 111: *Clyde Republican*, Clyde, Kansas, 28 December 1905.
14. Page 114: US Department of Agriculture, Office of Public Roads and Rural Engineering, Farmer's Bulletin 597, March 1917. Used with permission.

15. Page 117: Pam Coon, Poway, California. Used with permission.
16. Page 118: Pam Coon, Poway, California. Used with permission.
17. Page 124: Pam Coon, Poway, California. Used with permission.
18. Page 125: Julie Evans, Yucaipa, California. Used with permission.

Chapter 8

1. Page 128: Alamy.com Public Domain.
2. Page 133: *Aurora Searchlight*, Aurora, Kansas, 23 September 1920.

Bibliography

1. Page 134: Pam Coon, Poway, California. Used with permission.

Appendix B

1. Page 144: Pam Coon, Poway, California. Used with permission.

Appendix C

1. Page 160: Kent Archives, Kent, England. Used with permission.
2. Page 161: Kent Archives, Kent, England. Used with permission

Appendix D

1. Page 166: Pam Coon, Poway, California. Used with permission.

About the Author:

1. Page 185: © 2024, David Hayes, www.photoguppy.com. Author photo.
2. Page 186: Pam Coon, Poway, California. Used with permission.

About the Author

David Hayes is a freelance writer and award-winning photographer. Over several decades, he has contributed to national magazines, as well as international publishing houses. David holds two computer degrees. He uses his investigative and organizational skills, much like a detective, to unlock mysteries of history and genealogy.

As a photographer, David has traveled to nearly every continent, searching for rare and natural beauty from around the world.

David currently resides in Bangkok, Thailand, with his wife. He continues to indulge his passions for writing, photography, and traveling to new and exotic places.

Wallace Travis, son of Jessie Woodruff and Ulysses Grant Travis. c. 1920.

Index

Page numbers in **bold** refer to illustrations

A

Ames (KS) **75**, 79, 97
Andrews, G. W. 7
Aurora (KS) xiv, xv, **xviii**, **9**, 24, 34, 45, 49, 50, 51, **69**, 70, 102, 103, **107**, 113, 126, 129, **133**
Austin, Erma Vera (b. 1904) 82, 148
Austin, Harold L. (b. 1911) 148
Austin, Lawrence Woodruff (b. 1906) 82, 148
Austin, Ray 82, 148. *See also* Woodruff, Ethel

B

Booth, John Wilkes 38
Brown, Dan 89–90
Browning, Frank 17, 32–33
Buell, Cora 79, 147
Buffalo Bill 37

C

Campbell, Della. *See* Woodruff, Della
Campbell, Joseph 34, 74, 143
Campbell, Nellie (b. 1886) 40, 143
Campbell, Walter 34, 143
Canterbury (UK) 153, 154, 155, 158–59
Cartwright, Elizabeth 157, 158, 163, 165
Charles I 162
Chesebro, Ruth (b. 1922) 148
Chesebro, Wayne (b. 1918) 148
Chicago 21, 91, 108, 130
Cloud County (KS): environment of 4–5, 22–23, 26, 47, 51, 94, 129; history of 22, 24, 34, 37, 47, 94, 129, 132, 139; and Spanish Flu 94, 120; and World War I 115. *See also* Aurora; Clyde; Colfax; Concordia; Elk; Glasco; Huscher; Jamestown; Miltonvale; Minersville; Starr
Cloud, Colonel William 6
Clyde (KS) **vi–vii**, xvi, 2, 3, 5, 6–7, 8, 22, 34, 37, 38, 46, 50, 51, 59, **62**, 64, 75, 77, 78, 79, 82, 83, 84, 85, **92**, 96, 97, 104, 111, **111**, 112, 126
Colfax (KS) **v**, xvi, 16, 22, 23, 24, 25–26, 28, 32, 34, 39, 43, 45, 51, 59, 64, 80, 96, 103, 112
Concordia (KS) 2, 3, 7–8, **20**, 24, 34, **36**, 37, 43, 44, 45, 49, 50, 51, 53, 63, 64, 71, 77, 78, 79, **85**, 87, 88, 89, 94, 99, 100, 104, 108, 119, 121, 123
Corbett, Boston 38
Cranford-Westfield Woodruffs 169–170, 170n
Custer, General George 21

D

Domesday Book 154

E

Edison, Thomas 21
Elizabeth I 156
Elizabethtown (New Jersey) xiii, 169–71, 172
Elk (KS) 45, 75
English, William 7

F

Farmers' Alliance Party 43–44
Ford, Henry 49, 63, 93. *See also* Model T
Fordwich (UK) 11, 151, 152, 153, 154–59, 162, 166
Fox, James C. 74, 143
Fry, Ambrose Booten 77, 147
Fry, David (b. 1901) 147
Fry, Harley (b. 1919) 147
Fry, Thomas (b. 1907) 147
Fry, Vernon (b. 1902) 147

G

Glasco (KS) 24, 34, 103
Gosmer, John 158–59, **160**, 162–63, 165, 166–68, 170, 171
grasshopper plague 26–27

H

Hageman, James M. 5, 6–7
Hageman, James E. 89
Hawkins, Alma May (b. 1907) 74, 146
Hawkins, Clarence (b. 1909) 74, 146
Hawkins, James Franklin 74, 146
Heald Meat market 80, **81**
Henry VIII 153, 156
Heusted, Sarah 40
Hickok, Wild Bill 21
Homestead Act 5
Howe, Daniel 165, 166
Huscher, Carrie 40, 70, **71**, **134**, 144
Huscher (KS) xvi, 34, 40, 45, 53, 70+n, 74, 77, 102

J

Jamestown (KS) 24, 34, **48**, 88, 89
Jennings, Alice. *See* Woodruff, Alice
Jennings, Joshua 40
Jennings, Mary Elizabeth. *See* Woodruff, Mary
Johnson, Albert 123, **124**, 126, 131, 143
Johnson, Dorothy **35**

L

Long, Major Stephen 4, 23

M

mail. *See* postal service
Marlatt, Ella 88
Massachusetts Colony 11, 159, 163, 165
McClure, Harvey Russell (b. 1890) 144
McClure, Irving Clay (b. 1883) **164**, 144
McClure, Thomas 144, **164**
McKinley, William 63, 90
Miltonvale (KS) xvi, 34, 38, 44, 50, 51, 59, 64, 73, 82, 96, 121, 122, 130, 131
Minersville (KS) 24, 45
Model T xiv, 63, 93, 126
Mottin, Marie ("Mamie") 55, **73**, 146

N

Nation, Carrie. *See* prohibition

P

Peale, Ella 131
postal service xvi, 34, 77–79, 82–83, 97, 130. *See also* Woodruff, Anson; Woodruff, Edmond Silas
prairie fever 2–3
prohibition 50, 64, 108, 129

R

railroads xvi, 16, 27, 34, 38, 40, 44–45, 70n, 85, **85**, 87, 94

INDEX

Rebekahs. *See* Woodruff, Pearl
Republican River 3, **4**, 64, 78–79, 94
Ringling Brothers 49
Roosevelt, Theodore 63, 93
Rupe, John B. 6

S

Shakespeare, William 157
Shirley County 5, 6
Southampton (Long Island) xiii, 11, 151, 165–68, 169, 171
Spanish flu 94, 119–20
Spring Valley Farm 68, **69**
Springer, Sarah 87
Starr (KS) 21, 44, 45, 104

T

teaching. *See* Woodruff family: and education; Woodruff, Cesil; Woodruff, Cora May; Woodruff, David; Woodruff, Fannie Mariah; Woodruff, Grace; Woodruff, Harold H.; Woodruff, Lena Joanna; Woodruff, Ruth; Woodruff School
telephone service 50, 64, 70–72, 86–87
Travis, Bessie (b. 1893) 53, **54**, 146
Travis, Ortha (b. 1896) 53, 146
Travis, Ulysses G. 51, **52**, 53, 103, 121, 126, 146
Travis, Wallace Irving (b. 1904) 146, **184**
Truesdell family 8

W

Washington County (OH) 11, 22, 28, 33, 175–78
Watermelon Festival xvi, 50, 83
White Way (KS) 110, **110**
Will, Jenny 123+n, 131
Will, Moses 123, **125**, 131. *See also* Woodruff, Dorothea
Wonderland Theater (Concordia) 79, 99, 100
Woodroffe, John (b. 1574) 155
Woodroffe, Robert (d. 1611) 155, 156, 157
Woodroffe, William (d. 1587) 156
Woodrove, Thomas (b. 1508) 155–56
Woodruff family: in California xiv, 53n, 64–65, 66, 68, 74, 95, 111, 130, 131, 132, 132n; and education 101–07, 130, 139–41; emigration to America 163; in England 151–59; origin of name 152; and Spanish flu 120; weddings of 123–24, **124**; and World War I 115–16, 119. *See also* Cranford-Westfield; Elizabethtown; Fordwich; Southampton; Washington County; Woolley Manor
(*individual Woodruffs*)
Woodruff, Ada Maude (b. 1889) 40, 53, **71**, 72, 86, **134**, 144
Woodruff, Albert E. (b. 1865) 13, 40, 53, 70, **71**, 72, 86–87, 122, 130, **134**, 144
Woodruff, Albert (b. 1890) 53, 72, **117**, 130, 140, 145; in World War I 115–16
Woodruff, Alice (née Jennings) 40, 42, 72, 122, 126, 145
Woodruff, Allie Imogen (b. 1908) 80, 81, 82, 148
Woodruff, Alma (b. 1903) **i**, 66, 68, **106**, **107**, 131, 144
Woodruff, Alvin (b. 1903) **i**, 66, 68, **106**, **107**, 144
Woodruff, Amanda Loverna (b. 1893) 53, **71**, 86, 144
Woodruff, Anna A. (b. 1870) 13, 146
Woodruff, Anna Jane (née Neill) 17, 33, 59, 149
Woodruff, Annie May (b. 1884) 17, 46, 150
Woodruff, Anson (b. 1848) 11, 17, 24, 34, 123, 130, 149; as hunter 16, 59, 82–83; ill health of 83, 84, 122; and postal service 18, 78, 82–83; and military service 16–17, 46, 59, 83; and music 100; and public office 17, 24, 33, 46; and scandal 17, 32–33
Woodruff, Arthur Clyde (b. 1877) 15, 33, 77, 91, 112, 113, 115, 140, 147; and road maintenance 113, 130

Woodruff, Benjamin Franklin (b. 1909) 70, **71**, 145
Woodruff, Bennie (b. 1890) 17, 59, 150
Woodruff, Beulah F. (b. 1906) 70, **71**, 145
Woodruff, Beulah Luretta (b. 1905) 79, 100, 130, 147
Woodruff, Blanche (b. 1892) 53, **71**, 86, 144
Woodruff, Carl (b. 1873) 15, 33, 45, 147
Woodruff, Carl Edmond (b. 1915) 148
Woodruff, Cesil (b. 1896) **i**, 53, 68, **104**, **105**, **106**, 121+n, 144; relations with father 131; as teacher 102, 103, 140
Woodruff, Charles Oscar (b. 1928) 149
Woodruff, Charles Scott (b. 1888) 17, 46, 83, 112, 123, 130, 150; as football player 84, 111, **111**; and Spanish flu 120; in World War I 115
Woodruff, Clarence (b. 1908) 70, **71**, 145
Woodruff, Clark (b. 1871) 13, 33, **39**, 51, 55, **57**, 64, 72, **73**, 74, 112, 130, 132n, 146
Woodruff, Clive Donald (b. 1914) 147
Woodruff, Cora (b. 1864) 13, 64, 144, **164**. *See also* McClure, Thomas
Woodruff, Cora May (b. 1896) 53, 123, 126, 145; as teacher 102, 103, 140
Woodruff, David (b. 1845) 11, 15–16, 22, **29**, **31**, 32n, 33+n, 38, **39**,77, 82, 130, 132 **95**, 147; and coal 45; death of 96, 120, 122; as farmer 23, 28, 46, 75–76, **76**, 84; military service 15; in public office 16, 24–26, 43–44, 45–46, 58–59, 59n, 74–75, 80, 108; as teacher 15, 16, 25, 44, 59, 102, 139, 140
Woodruff, David Anson (b. 1927) 149
Woodruff, Della (b. 1858) 13, 34, **39**, 40, 74, 130, 143
Woodruff, Dorothea ("Dolly") (b. 1901) **i**, 66, **105**, **106**, **107**, **125**, 131, 144
Woodruff, Dora (b. 1879) 13, 33, **39**, 55, 64, 74, 146. *See also* Hawkins, James Franklin
Woodruff, Doris Nola (b. 1905) 80, 148
Woodruff, Edith (b. 1913) 147
Woodruff, Edmond Silas (b. 1878) xiii, 16, 34, 38, 147, 175; administers father's estate 96, 122; arrested 126; as businessman 97, **98**; guardian to nieces 82, 122; as Mason 79, 112; and politics 108; and postal service 18, 77–79, 83, 96–97, 113, 119; as singer 79, 99, **99**, 112; and Spanish flu 120
Woodruff, Emmette (b. 1882) 16, 45, 80, 148; disappearance of 81–82, 121–22; partner in Heald market 80–81
Woodruff, Esther (b. 1899) 53, 91, 102n, 104, 130, 145
Woodruff, Ethel Leona (b. 1884) 16, 45, 82, 148. *See also* Austin, Ray
Woodruff, Fannie Mariah (b. 1895) 18, 59, 112, 139–40, 150; as teacher 102, 103, 119, 140
Woodruff, Fannie Mildred (b. 1923) 149
Woodruff, Florence (b. 1860) 13, 74, 143
Woodruff, Gene (b. 1910) 149
Woodruff, George Albert (b. 1890) 53, **71**, 86, 120, 123, 144; auto mechanic 108–09, 111; race car driver 108; drives White Way 110; and World War I 115
Woodruff, Gladys (b. 1904) 80, 148
Woodruff, Grace (b. 1892) 53, 72, 120, 126, 145; as teacher 102, 103, 104, 113, 122, 141
Woodruff, Harold H. (b. 1898) 53, 72, 86, 91, 113, **118**, 122, 126, 145; as teacher 104, 112, 141; in World War I 115
Woodruff, Hazel (b. 1895) 53, **71**, 72, 86, 91, 119, 141, 144
Woodruff, Hildred (b. 1904) 70, **71**, 122, 145
Woodruff, Hiram (b. 1835) **29**, **30**, 38–40, **39**, **65**, 143; in California 64–65, 74, 95; as farmer 12, 15, 23, 27–28, 51, 52, 75; to Kansas 13; military service 12, 51, 65; in public office 24
Woodruff, Hiram H. (b. 1894) 53, 112, 113, 123, 145; in World War I 115
Woodruff, Howard (b. 1918) 149
Woodruff, Isaac (b. 1862) **9**, 13, 40, 53, 64, 66, **67**, 68, **69**, 70, 102, 108, 112, 120,

121n, 126, 131, **133**, 143
Woodruff, James Anson (b. 1878) 17, 34, 84, 85, 91, 149
Woodruff, James Roscoe (b. 1915) 149
Woodruff, James William (b. 1913) 145
Woodruff, Jesse 87–88
Woodruff, Jessie (b. 1874) 13, 33, 51, **52**, 53, 126, 146. *See also* Travis, Ulysses G.
Woodruff, Joseph (b. 1899) **i**, 53, **106**, **107**, 115, 123, 131, 144
Woodruff, Joseph Duane (b. 1905) 147
Woodruff, Joshua (Josiah) (b. 1905) 145
Woodruff, Julius (b. 1900) 72, **73**, 115, 130, 146
Woodruff, Leah Anna (b. 1903) 80, 82, 148
Woodruff, Lena Alice (b. 1920) 149
Woodruff, Lena Joanna (b. 1892) 17, 59, 79, 84, **101**, 124, 130, 150; as musician 100, 112; as teacher 100, 102, 104, 141
Woodruff, Leslie Scott (b. 1922) 150
Woodruff, Lewis (b. 1868) 13, 42, **42**, 53, 72, 112, 122, 126, 145
Woodruff, Lillian Victoria (b. 1907) 79, 147
Woodruff, Livinia ("Linnie" b. 1876) 13, 33, **39**, 51, 55, **56**, 146
Woodruff, Lulu May ("June") (b. 1874) 15, 33, 58, 77, 147; accidentally shot by husband 77. *See also* Fry, Ambrose Booten
Woodruff, Margaret (b. 1870) 13, 146
Woodruff, Mariette (b. 1932) 150
Woodruff, Mark 87, 88–91; arrested 90
Woodruff, Mary Elizabeth (b. 1866 née Jennings) 40, 53, 66, 68, 70, 120–21, 131, 140, 141, 143
Woodruff, Mary Jane (b. 1920) 150
Woodruff, Mary Maude (née McDonald) 141, 147
Woodruff, Matthew 87+n
Woodruff, Mildred G. (b. 1907) 141, 147
Woodruff, Nancy (b. 1930) 150
Woodruff, Naomi (b. 1905) 72, 126, 145
Woodruff, Neil Parker (b. 1920) 150
Woodruff, Ova (b. 1888) **xii**, 40, **41**, 53, 120, 143
Woodruff, Pearl Lena (b. 1891) 16, 58, 102n, 112, 123, 141, 148
Woodruff, Rachel (b. 1899) 53, **71**, 145
Woodruff, Richard Scott (b. 1914) 149
Woodruff, Ruby (née Woodworth) 80, 81, 82, 121, 148
Woodruff, Ruth (b. 1894) **i**, 53, 68, **104**, **106**, 121, 123, **124**, 126, 131, 143; as teacher 102–03, 140, 141
Woodruff, Sarah Amanda (née Gilmore) 13, **14**, **39**, **65**, 74, 143
Woodruff, Sarah Ann (b. 1924) 149
Woodruff, Seth Rees (b. 1901) 70, **71**, 145
Woodruff, Silas (b. 1813) 11–12, 13, 15, 74, 177, 178
Woodruff, Silas (b. 1882) 17, 46, 84, 85–86, 91, 123, 150; robbed 86
Woodruff, Silas Wayne (b. 1934) 150
Woodruff, Timothy (b. 1897) **i**, 53, **106**, 120, 144
Woodruff, Victoria (née Browning) 15, 32n, 45, 58, 96, 147
Woodruff, William (b. 1879) 17, 34, 130, 149
Woodruff, William Byron (b. 1924) 150
Woodruff, William Cordell (b. 1916) 149
Woodruff, Zaccheus (b. 1898) 53, 70, 144
Woodruff School 16, 25, 44, 59, 102, 130, 132, 140, 141
Woodworth, Curtis W. 80
Woolley Manor 152
World War I 94, 114–16, 119, 140. *See also* Woodruff family

Z

Zahn, William 21

www.ingramcontent.com/pod-product-compliance
Lightning Source LLC
Chambersburg PA
CBHW040236110526
44582CB00021B/210/J